D1062091

PROPERTY OF
FORT WAYNE
ART INSTITUTE
LIBRARY
1026 W. BERRY ST.
FORT WAYNE, IND.

THE LIFE OF BERNINI

VITA
DEL CAVALIERE
GIO. LORENZO BERNINO
SCULTORE, ARCHITETTO, E PITTORE,

SCRITTA DA

FILIPPO BALDINUCCI FIORENTINO.

ALLA SACRA, E REALE MAESTA'

DI

CRISTINA
REGINA DI SUEZIA.

IN FIRENZE, nella Stamperia di Vincenzio Vangelisti.

Con licenza de' Superiori. MDCLXXXII.

THE LIFE OF BERNINI

BY

FILIPPO BALDINUCCI

TRANSLATED FROM THE ITALIAN BY

CATHERINE ENGGASS

FOREWORD BY ROBERT ENGGASS

The Pennsylvania State University Press

University Park and London 1966

LIBRARY OF CONGRESS CATALOG CARD NUMBER: 65–26094

PRINTED IN THE UNITED STATES OF AMERICA

DESIGNED BY MARILYN SHOBAKEN

CONTENTS

FOREWORD

Filippo Baldinucci's biography is our principal source for the life of Bernini, the protean genius of Baroque art, who did more than any other man to shape the image of Rome as we see it today. Queen Christina of Sweden commissioned the book and provided for its publication in 1682, only two years after Bernini's death. That she chose as her author none of the art critics, theorists, or historians then active in Rome, but Baldinucci from Florence, gives some idea of the prestige this writer was beginning to enjoy in the artistic and literary circles of his day.

What we know of Baldinucci's life comes largely from the biography written by his son, Francesco Saverio, which remained in manuscript form until its publication by Sergio Samek Ludovici in 1948. This biography traces the family back to 1378 when Giovanni Maria Baldinucci held the office of magistrate of the Tuscan Republic. Filippo Baldinucci was born on 13 June 1624. His father Giovanni, a merchant, put his education in the hands of the Jesuits, who must have contributed to the deeply religious outlook that was to remain with him throughout his life. For a time he assisted his father in business. Later he studied under the engraver and wood carver, Jacopo Maria Foggini, and then with the painter Matteo Rosselli. Although he soon abandoned painting, he continued to draw all his life. It was his portrait sketches that seem to have won him *entrée* into the circle of aristocrats and art patrons that gathered around Alessandro Valori at the Villa d'Empoli Vecchio.

Shortly after his father's death in 1656 Baldinucci married, but not before going through the rigors of St. Ignatius' *Spiritual Ex-*

ercises to determine if he should immerse himself fully in worldly affairs. Five sons were born of this marriage. The intensely religious atmosphere of this household, so emphasized in Francesco Saverio's biography, is at least partially confirmed by the religious vocation of three of his sons. Baldinucci's firstborn, Giovanni Filippo, was a Dominican monk who lived first at Fiesole and then at S. Marco's in Florence where he was a curate. His fourth son, Isidoro, was a parish priest. His youngest, Antonio, achieved distinction as a Jesuit missionary. On 16 April 1893 he was beatified by Pope Leo XIII.

Baldinucci's growing reputation brought him to the attention of Ferdinand II de' Medici, Archduke of Florence, who in 1664 sent him to his sister, the Archduchess Anna of Austria, to put in order properties that formed a part of her dowry and were kept at the Virgiliana in Mantua. At the same time he had an opportunity to study the famous painting collection of the Gonzagas, thus broadening his understanding of Northern Italian art.

Baldinucci's advancement in court circles and the real recognition of his talent in the realm of connoisseurship came about under Ferdinand's son, Cardinal Leopoldo de' Medici, a brilliant intellectual who as ruler of Tuscany was famous for his encouragement of literature, the visual arts, and scientific research. Leopoldo was, *inter alia,* the guiding light of the Accademia del Cimento (founded in 1657) which is generally considered to have been the prototype for the Académie des sciences in Paris and the Royal Society in London. He assigned Baldinucci the task of putting in order the vast collection of drawings which the Medici family had been assembling for generations. After having given the Duke proof of his extraordinary ability to distinguish one hand from another on the basis of style, an area in which he was certainly a pioneer, Baldinucci classified each drawing by artist and added brief information as to dating. He also bought many new drawings for the Duke. Today they form the nucleus of the Gabinetto dei Disegni of the Uffizi, one of the greatest collections in the world. This interest in ordering and classifying, growing out of an atmosphere favorable to both art and science, had obvious significance in terms of the development, still well in the future, of art history as a formal discipline.

Baldinucci's next task was to rearrange the Medici collection of paintings and to add to it works by artists not previously represented. Here again the idea of building a collection that would be comprehensive and representative was something quite new. Baldinucci was also instrumental in forming a gallery of self-portraits, first by bringing together in a single hall the examples that previously had been scattered throughout the collection, then by adding to them self-portraits of contemporary painters. This world famous collection is now in the Uffizi.

The capstone of Baldinucci's career is his encyclopedic history of painters, sculptors, and architects, the *Notizie de' professori del disegno da Cimabue in quà,* published in six large volumes, the first of which appeared in 1681 and the last, posthumously, in 1728. This project was a direct outgrowth of Baldinucci's work in classifying and building the Medici collections. He began with the enthusiastic encouragement of Leopoldo de' Medici, but the Cardinal's death in 1675 ended his financial support and retarded the work's completion.

In his *Notizie* Baldinucci deals with the visual arts as a continual progression. He begins late in the thirteenth century with Cimabue and ends late in the seventeenth with Mattia Preti. He traces closely the derivation of one master's style from another. Baldinucci turns for his model to the lives of the artists which Vasari had written more than a century before. It was his explicit intention to expand Vasari's work and bring it up to date. Baldinucci began by looking backward, but he ended by moving forward with such strides that his *Notizie* is now recognized as a major step in the development of the history of art. He had a passion for source materials not equalled until the nineteenth century. He checked his facts against all sorts of archival data: account books, notarial records, diaries, chronicles, and the like. He even drew up and sent to living artists questionnaires, some of which still survive, filled out with the answers, in the National Library in Florence. Rejecting Vasari's Tuscan provincialism, he surveyed all the Italian schools—Venetian, Lombard, Neapolitan, Bolognese—and passed beyond the Alps (with the help of Karl van Mander and others) to create, as Julius Schlosser says, the first universal history of the visual arts in Europe.

Baldinucci's fascination not only with art but also with language is demonstrated by his dictionary of art terms, the *Vocabolario toscano dell'arte del disegno,* which he published in Florence in 1681. A work of impressive scope, it deals with the major arts as well as with artisan-work and trades. It clarifies the language of the studio and defines the terminology of artists' handbooks. It is the first book of its type and was absolutely definitive in its day. Through this work as well as through his *Notizie,* Baldinucci gained membership in the Accademia della Crusca, an honor that signified recognition both as a scholar and man of letters. The Accademia della Crusca or Academy of the Chaff was founded in Florence late in the sixteenth century expressly to study, inventory, and perfect the Italian language. The academy's device was a sieve in which the members figuratively sifted words in order to separate the acceptable from the unacceptable. The crowning achievement of this organization was the publication in 1612, after more than twenty years of work, of a dictionary of Italian: *Vocabolario degli Accademici della Crusca.* It, therefore, preceded the *Dictionnaire* of the *Académie française* by about eighty years. The Accademia della Crusca is still in existence and has maintained, over the centuries, its position as the guardian of the linguistic purity of Italian.

Baldinucci's last major work was his *Cominciamento e progresso dell'arte dell'intagliare in rame,* a history of etching and engraving that was published in Florence in 1686. It is notable as the first serious history of prints appearing at the time when this art form was just beginning to receive recognition as an independent field. Baldinucci makes a conscientious effort to survey the history of this medium throughout Europe. It is no accident that he begins with Dürer who impressed him greatly, though the German's style was too foreign to him to provide any basis for empathy. Rembrandt is dutifully included, though Baldinucci had not even the vaguest sense of his grandeur. He praises him as an "umorista di prima classe"!

Baldinucci's *Lettera a Vincenzo Capponi,* a brief essay published in Rome in 1681, is of interest for its serious attempt, two centuries before Morelli, to establish specific criteria through which the style of one master can be distinguished from another and the original work of art from the copy. In *La Veglia, o Dialogo di Sincero Veri,* which appeared first in Lucca in 1684, he stressed the ascendancy of Florentine art while at the same time depreciating Malvasia's efforts to promote the Bolognese School. The book remains of interest for its discussion of the importance and use of documentation.

Two formal lectures that Baldinucci delivered at the Accademia della Crusca during the winter of 1690–91 were devoted to a rather tedious comparison of ancient and modern painting with arguments as to which was better. (Modern won.) They were published in Florence the following year under the title *Lezione di Filippo Baldinucci nell'Accademia della Crusca.* Baldinucci also wrote a series of short farces or one-act plays that deal with humorous situations in which Tuscan peasants become involved with the bourgeoisie: lawyers, notaries, landlords, and the like. They were probably never intended for publication, but a few of these *Lazzi contadineschi* appeared in print in the nineteenth century.

Toward the end of his life Baldinucci assembled a new collection of over one thousand drawings, replacing an earlier group he gave or sold to the Medici. These were subsequently acquired by Pandolfo Pandolfini and eventually, in 1806, by the Louvre where they are now.

From the death in 1675 of his greatest patron, Cardinal Leopoldo de' Medici, Baldinucci had been plagued by a lack of funds for his scholarly undertakings. By 1688, for example, only three volumes of his *Notizie* had been published. This must have contributed to the melancholia that, according to his son, clouded the last years of his life and ultimately brought on the dropsy that caused his death on New Year's Day, 1697.

Apart from his monumental *Notizie de' professori del disegno da Cimabue in quà,* Baldinucci's most important publication is his life of Bernini. The *Vita del Cavaliere Gio. Lorenzo Bernino scultore, architetto e pittore* was published in Florence in 1682. From that time on it was never forgotten. The biography forms a part of the edition of Baldinucci's works in ten volumes that Domenico Maria Manni brought out in Florence, 1767–74. It is included in the edition of "Classici italiani" edited by Carpani and published in Milan, 1811–12. A. Burda and O. Pollak edited a new edition with a German translation and abundant commentary, based on notes left by Alois Riegl and published in Vienna in 1912. The most recent Italian edition is that by Sergio Samek Ludovici published in Rome in 1948 with copious notes, an excellent introduction, and numerous illustrations.

Another early biography of Bernini, published by his son in 1713, has in general been much less favorably received. Schlosser says that Domenico Bernini surveys "the artistic creations of his famous father virtually without understanding them, so that his work remains much inferior to that of the connoisseur Baldinucci, on which he draws copiously without citing." Concerning Bernini's trip to France we have biographical material of an entirely different order. Sieur de Chantelou, a French nobleman whom the King appointed to serve as Bernini's guide and honor guard, was an acute observer with firsthand knowledge of the Italian scene and a highly developed artistic sensibility. The daily entries in his diary, extending from early June through mid-October of 1665, provide us with a more penetrating analysis of Bernini as an individual than any other source, despite the brevity of the period covered.

Early in 1681, only a few months after Bernini's death, Baldinucci came down to Rome to enter his son, Antonio, who was then fifteen years old, in the Jesuit Novitiate on the Quirinal. At this time Queen Christina of Sweden asked Baldinucci, whom she already knew by reputation, to visit her and discuss the publication of a biography of Bernini. Christina presumably provided the funds that made possible the publication of his life of Bernini, and he dedicated it to her. The opening pages of the book, which Baldinucci fills with the most extravagant praises of the Queen and her talents, are not entirely figments of Baroque hyperbole. She was an extraordinary woman.

Christina was the daughter of King Gustavus Adolphus of Sweden, a great military leader and scourge of the Catholic armies during the Thirty Years' War. In 1633 Gustavus died in battle leaving Christina as his sole heir and a Queen-elect. From childhood she demonstrated a passion for learning. After becoming reigning sovereign at eighteen, she assembled about her scholars and writers from all over Europe, among them Voss, Brochart, and Descartes. For a brief period, under the guidance of this brilliant woman, Stockholm became the most important intellectual center of Europe. Under Christina's reign education, science, and literature flourished; but her secret conversion to Catholicism, then forbidden in Sweden, forced her to abdicate in 1654. Most of her remaining years were spent in Rome. There she was welcomed with triumphant processions. Her conversion was hailed as a great symbolic victory for the Catholic Restoration. In the Papal City, where Christina continued her interest in politics, her influence made itself felt on occasion in the College of Cardinals. But her strongest and most lasting imprint upon Rome was in the field of the arts. The men of letters and artists that she gathered about her at her palace on the Lungara formed the nucleus of what was to become the Arcadia, the most important literary and scientific society in Rome. Christina was famous for her discriminating taste in all the arts. Her painting collection contained works by Perugino and Raphael, Titian and Tintoretto, Rubens and Van Dyck. She was the first important patron of the great composer Alessandro Scarlatti, who became her *maestro di cappella.* Another noted composer, Arcangelo Corelli, was director of her orchestra. Christina was a friend and admirer of Bernini, for whose work she had an unbounded admiration. She owned his *Salvator Mundi,* a major piece of sculpture entirely by his hand, now unfortunately lost.

Bernini died rich in wealth and fame, but somewhat under a cloud as a result of allegations, today considered false, that the work he had done on the niches of the piers at the crossing of St. Peter's had weakened these piers thus threatening the stability of the great dome. At the request of the Queen, chiefly as an affirmation of Bernini's greatness, but also as a defense against these attacks, Baldinucci undertook this work. He makes it perfectly clear in the epilogue of the book that he wishes to write only good things about Bernini and his career. The unsuccessful results of Bernini's trip to Paris are passed over in silence. The mutilation of his colossal equestrian statue of Louis XIV was not to take place until 1688, but the antagonism that he engendered at the French court was already very real. There is no hint that Bernini's plans to rebuild the Louvre met with bitter opposition, above all from Colbert, and that shortly after he returned to Rome his project was abandoned, never to be resumed. Baldinucci presents Borromini as a student and assistant of Bernini, who by criticism of the master reveals himself as an ingrate. Today he is considered to have been at times Bernini's collaborator rather than his assistant—one who owed the master little and was able to emerge as an independent architect only after Bernini fell temporarily into disgrace (this too Baldinucci minimizes) following the death of Urban VIII.

This is not in any sense to imply that Baldinucci's biography is fiction. On the contrary, it is, for its time, an extraordinarily accurate and objective account; in certain areas it is a model of historical methodology. For his detailed defense of Bernini in the controversy surrounding the dome and the domical piers of St. Peter's, Baldinucci made an intensive study of all the relevant documents preserved in the archives of the Fabbrica of St. Peter's: plans and elevations made by Bramante, Baldassare Peruzzi, Antonio da San Gallo, Michelangelo, and Carlo Maderno. He examined the minutes of the committee meetings dealing with these matters and recorded in the *Libri congregationum.* He read letters written by Bernini to his architectural assistants and studied Bernini's own records. He consulted at length with living architects and architectural engineers, above all with Mattia de' Rossi, who then held the post of chief architect of St. Peter's. He carried out the most detailed examination of the fabric of the building itself; he took measurements and studied wall surfaces in the passageways in the piers, in the spaces within and outside of the double shell of the dome, around the drum and the lantern, and in the adjacent areas, always checking his findings with experts. Authorities today fully support Baldinucci's conclusions. His investigation of the circumstances surrounding the demolition of Bernini's bell tower—a project which if carried through would have so beautifully framed St. Peter's dome and gone so far to restore the equilibrium lost when Maderno extended the facade—is only slightly less thorough. Baldinucci's biography also includes the texts of a number of letters that are in themselves documents: letters from prominent figures such as Louis XIV; Cardinal Mazarin, his Prime Minister; Colbert, his Minister of Finance; Father Oliva, the General of the Jesuit Order; and from Bernini himself.

Another reflection of this same spirit of painstaking research is the lengthy catalogue of Bernini's works that Baldinucci appends to his biography. Since these lists include a large number of works that are now lost, they are particularly valuable to those students of Bernini who wish to enlarge the corpus of his known work. In view of the remarkable discoveries that have been made since World War II by Italo Faldi and others, we have every reason to expect further progress in this area.

But beyond Baldinucci's interest in documentation and authentication, one of the things that makes his narrative ring true and raises it above the level of a mere compilation is the fact that he was a highly skilled connoisseur with a keen eye for style. When he writes of the expression of "rightful wrath" on the face of Bernini's *David,* with its "powerful knitted brows, the terrible fixity of the eyes, and the upper jaw clamped tightly over the lower lip," he does so on the basis of close observation and with genuine enthusiasm. In discussing Bernini's fountains he describes the sculpture, but he also notes the pleasing effect of the murmuring waters. His own experience both as a graphic artist and a connoisseur accounts for his profound admiration of Bernini's skill in *disegno.* Unlike most of the critics of his age, he understands and admires the Baroque, as Samek Ludovici points out. He praises Bernini for drawing together the separate arts of sculpture, painting, and architecture. He admires his ability to pass beyond the rules and create his own. Bernini's theatrical quality, his sense of surprise, appeals to him. In discussing the Four Rivers Fountain, Baldinucci reveals that he is much impressed by the way in which Bernini hollowed out the center of the rock mass on all four sides so that the huge granite obelisk set on top of it seems to rest on air. In the tomb of Alexander VII he admires the way in which Bernini takes the awkward doorway at the back of the chapel and integrates it so completely with the whole composition that what was a liability becomes an asset. In the tomb of Urban VIII he notes with surprise and delight how Death, having just turned the page inscribed with the name of the Barberini Pope, holds up the edge so that we can make out beneath part of the name of his predecessor, Pope Gregory XV. In discussing Bernini's theatrical productions it is the dramatic staging devices that particularly catch Baldinucci's attention: the water that seems about to engulf the audience in the spectacle of the inundation of the Tiber; or the production in which the whole stage seems to catch fire, to the terror of the spectators.

Baldinucci's book is a seventeenth-century biography of a seventeenth-century artist. As such it is of value for the glimpses it gives us of the Papal City in this period of resurgent Catholicism when the popes and their followers were noted for their splendor. Bernini's career is tightly interwoven with the artistic programs of the reigning pontiffs, many of whom were his good friends, with the papal nephews, and with the glittering court circles that most of the rulers of the Papal States gathered around them during the heyday of nepotism. His patrons were the Borghese, the Barberini, the Pamphili, the Chigi, the Rospigliosi, the Altieri—names still richly resonant in Rome for the memory of their lavish embellishment of the Holy City. Nor is it all glitter. Baldinucci finds himself occasionally forced to mention some of the intrigues that flourished in the court circles surrounding Rome's absolutist rulers. But he loses no opportunity to stress the status of the artist through his close association with the great and the near great. In this respect the careers of Bernini and Rubens offer many interesting points of comparison. Those with some knowledge of European history can, by reading between the lines, find reflections of some of the great issues that confronted the papacy during this crucial period. Thus the almost pathetic eagerness of Father Oliva, the head of the Jesuit Order, to please and flatter Louis XIV, above all by sending a reluctant Bernini off to Paris, is a reflection of the strength of the Gallican movement, which sought at every opportunity to make the Catholic Church subservient to French national policy, and threatened to establish in France a separate national church like that in England.

Baldinucci himself was very much a product of the Counter Reformation. According to his son, Francesco Saverio, the strong religious vocation of his children was a reflection of their father's own deep piety. Antonio Baldinucci, the son of Filippo who was later beatified, is quoted as saying to his brothers gathered round their father's deathbed, "filii sanctorum sumus." For Baldinucci art is the result of divine inspiration operating through man, and the work of art is a natural outgrowth of the life of the artist. This viewpoint accounts for the stress he lays on Bernini's own piety, as well as for the moralistic digressions that are scattered throughout the book. It probably also explains his attitude of *nihil nisi bonum* and his correlative dislike of polemics and those who polemicize.

FOREWORD

While today we value Baldinucci chiefly for what he has to say, it would be a shame to ignore altogether how he says it. More than one modern critic has noted the "impeccable style" of his prose. It is Baroque writing, far different from the kind of writing we are used to today, but for that very reason it helps broaden our understanding of the age. The long, rolling sentences, filled with subordinate clauses, are rich in internal rhythms. Baldinucci seeks to express his ideas with a multiplicity of terms, with a sparkling array of synonyms that at times will strike the modern reader as prolix, but that can also be eloquent.

In the seventeenth century many great writers made use of these elements of style. We are reminded in English, for example, of Robert Burton's *Anatomy of Melancholy* or Thomas Browne's *Hydriotaphia*. When Baldinucci admires the abundance of ornament on Bernini's baldachin in St. Peter's, he is predisposed to like it by analogy with the ornamentation of his own prose. The richness of his long periodic sentences, with elements at times carefully arranged in balanced parallels, is a literary counterpart of the garments of Bernini's figures, with their endless folds carefully arranged to produce complex but highly unified rhythms. Both are fully Baroque, reflecting an ebullient enthusiasm and the zest of the spirit.

R. E.

Baton Rouge, Louisiana
September 1965

THE LIFE OF
BERNINI

HOLY ROYAL MAJESTY

I have always believed it to be true, Your Majesty, indeed, most true, that of all the worldly joys that could ever appear desirable in our eyes, there is nothing more desirable than honor. For through honor man becomes almost larger than himself and in seeking the esteem and veneration of other men he can also, sometimes, to the extent of his own reputation, not only make brighter the fame of his ancestors, make greater the stature of his relatives, make more noble his posterity, but can make more glorious as well the very country that gave him birth—something that riches and other gifts of fortune cannot attain. If what I have said is accepted as true, it is necessary to profess openly that great monarchs (among which Your Majesty so gloriously stands out) chosen by Heaven from among thousands, and destined to crowns, to kingdoms and on whom Heaven bestows the fullness of every honor—that such monarchs are all required through inevitable law to contribute to honor. They do not possess nor can they possess any greater treasure with which to enrich others than honor itself. Therefore, one must, in truth, affirm that the noblest glory of their dignity and the most enviable (if indeed one is permitted the utterance) is not the power to make others rich, but the power to make them honored.

If one considers which are the virtues of this heavenly gift that are rendered most abundantly to Your Majesty, certainly they are to be found in the admirable qualities of your mind and the vast erudition of your most brilliant intellect. So much are you venerated by all, that there remains doubt as to which of Your Majesty's most noble attributes has the merit of pre-eminence;

whether it be the great distinction of your learning or the great sublimity of your royal state. All this I have well deliberated. On the other hand, Your Majesty's act of royal generosity in accepting one of such slight talent as myself to write of the deeds of Cavalier Giovan Lorenzo Bernini, a man who was not only extraordinary in sculpture, architecture, and painting, but eminent in other excellent faculties, is, upon attentive reflection, as much as to say that it pleased Your Majesty that I put my poor pen to the test of composing sentences that to be of service have need of the substance of Your Majesty's lofty thoughts. I do not know quite how to describe the confusion I have experienced and still experience in seeing myself, thanks to the benign hand of Your Highness, in possession of the most valuable honor that could ever come to me. Although it cannot be denied that in confrontation with the great merit of Your Majesty, the work is in itself small, yet, whatever it may lack, it is linked to the most sublime quality adorning the spirit of Your Majesty: the incessant craving for new and fine information to enrich the increasingly vast treasure of your noble intellect. I am not a little distressed by my awareness of the slight value that my skill was able to contribute to this work. Yet, the consolation I gain by turning my mind's eye to the honor Your Majesty has done me (which, however, relates to yourself and your royal nature and not to me) exceeds my distress by far. The same awareness would, indeed, have restrained me from placing my writings under the most learned eyes of Your Majesty—apart from your most kind command—were it not for the knowledge that in no way could I by chance be able to merit the generous gratification of Your Majesty, other than by the pure and simple account of the works of such a great virtuoso as was the Cavalier Bernini. The dignity of his works will, in my opinion, have no less power to draw the loving glances of Your Majesty than they will have to annihilate through their brilliance the obscurity of my prose. Deign, then, Your Majesty, to receive this my labor, whatever it may be, as a token of my most humble and prompt obedience. And if, by any chance, you should find something in it that merits approbation, attribute it, Your Majesty, to your own virtue, which, by condescending to honor me, first by having sent to me your most revered commands through the letter of the very worthy prelate, and then confirming them by voice, gave to my studies life, stimulus, spirit, and to my weakness, vigor. And here, prostrated at your feet, I dedicate myself forever to Your Holy Royal Majesty.

Florence, 5 November 1681

Your Most Humble, Most Devoted, and Most Obligated Servant,

FILIPPO BALDINUCCI

Marvelous, and almost like a miracle, is the strength of those hidden seeds which nature, ever the wise guardian of her finest elements, providentially sows and instills into the spirits of finer temper and loftier purpose, as into receptive and willing ground. Nor, in my opinion, does it seem extraordinary to those who look with more subtle discernment into the essence of things, that, inasmuch as they are of a heavenly line and united to our nature, these seeds by virtue of the place where they originated and their heritage of immortality can also vaunt the most intimate affinity to Heaven. It is reasonable that, as in cultivated ground, such a seed settles and flourishes with all its force in our minds in the same way that seeds quickly sprout up from the earth and within a brief period produce an abundant harvest of innumerable ears of grain when sown in good and well-chosen land. Such an effect, though seen to a greater or lesser degree in all mankind, is clearer and more sharply defined in those who have been destined and selected by nature to do great and wonderful deeds. The spirits of those of purer and nobler clay, whether they in fact be jewels of greater brilliance and higher worth or gems set in gold, shine through the body almost as a ray of light shines through glass. One sees, at times, a few individuals whose spirit from the dawn of their lives flashes forth from their eyes in such abundance and so blazingly that the strongest pupils cannot sustain the light or even its reflection. It seems that the whole spirit actually appears at the windows of the countenance, disdaining to mingle with matter and revealing, notwithstanding the body, a hint of its most secret beauties by signs, glances, words and motions.

In our time such strong and noble vitality of nature was the lot of Cavalier Giovan Lorenzo Bernini, a man who in the arts of painting, sculpture and architecture was not only great but extraordinary. To be ranked with the most splendid and renowned masters of antiquity and of modern times, he lacked little from fortune save the age.

But just as the marble blocks, which, thanks to his chisel, live and breathe in Rome and in many other parts of the world, might have remained mute and solitary in the native rock had not the master subjected them to the control of his implacable will, so Bernini's great creative power would have, to the same degree, I believe, been dissipated in the dash of youth and the license natural to those years had he not, almost from birth, placed himself under the unremitting pressure of the most rigorous study and application. It is a demonstration of the maxim that great talent improperly guarded will, like the transitory essence of flowers which, when distilled into a liqueur and placed in an inadequately sealed jar, evaporate within a few hours because of its extreme evanescence. The justice Bernini did himself by advantageously using the distinguished gifts of his spirit, granted to him by special grace, is shown very clearly by the enormous number of outstanding works that he executed.

If the length of his life were to be measured by these works, it could truly be reckoned to be very long; if by the years he actually lived, not short; but if measured by the longing of men and the entire world, then most brief. Although he himself made a living history and has no need of a written testimony for future centuries, nevertheless, to honor virtue and as an incentive it is fitting to relate something about him for posterity. I shall attempt to be very succinct. My aim is not to win fame for my pen by these writings but rather to bind myself to future generations who will I am certain envy our good fortune in having seen, thanks to Bernini, these three most noble arts maintained in rightful possession of their ancient dignity to which they were restored by the never sufficiently praised Michelangelo after their almost total collapse.

Pietro Bernini, the father of the artist, was a man of no small acclaim in painting and sculpture. He left his native Florence when he was a youth to study those arts in Rome. There, under the direction of Giuseppe d'Arpino and in the service of Cardinal Alessandro Farnese and many others, he worked meritoriously in both professions. Since his works have been written of by others and his accomplishments are well known, it is not incumbent on me to speak of them.

Impelled by the hope of greater opportunities, Pietro went to Naples where he married Angelica Galante, a Neapolitan. In addition to other children, he had by her a son born on December 7, 1598, whom he named Giovan Lorenzo. He is the one of whom we now speak. In truth he was born by divine plan, this child who, for Italy's good fortune, was to bring illumination to two centuries. In him it seemed that nature deliberately employed all her powers, so beautiful and intense was the spirit and so corruscating and impressive was the talent with which she adorned him. Nature made it easy for him to acquire his father's skills. He was so extraordinarily pleasing, that at the age of eight he made a small marble head of a child that was the marvel of everyone. Since the fame of his father's skill increased and resounded ever more clearly throughout Italy, Paul V, when he wanted such a master to execute the marble group he planned to have placed on the facade of the Pauline Chapel, requested and obtained Pietro's services from the viceroy.

Thus Pietro arrived in Rome with all his numerous family and established his residence. Here, in the world's most celebrated capital, a larger arena opened for the exultant flights of Giovan Lorenzo's genius. Only in that city could one admire the most celebrated works of ancient and modern painters and sculptors as well as the precious remains of ancient architecture which in spite of time, not an inconsiderable enemy, still stood miraculously in glorious ruin. Thus it was made easy for Bernini, through close and continuous study of the most praiseworthy works, above all those of the great Michelangelo and Raphael, to grasp the essence of all their perfection and distinction so that he could, in accordance with his ability, emulate the lofty ideas of those sublime spirits.

To this end, Bernini spent three continuous years from dawn until the sounding of the Ave Maria in the rooms of the Vatican drawing the objects of greatest rarity, those with qualities of excellence and exoticism as well as examples from antiquity. He tried with all his power to arrive at an exact likeness and quickly gained such fame that men spoke of him in the Roman academies as an incredible marvel, something never before seen. The first work to emerge from his chisel in Rome was a marble head that was placed in the Church of S. Potenziana. Bernini had then scarcely completed his tenth year.

Paul V, greatly impressed by the acclaim aroused by such merit, wished to see the youth. He had him brought before him and asked him as a jest, if he could sketch a head. Giovan Lorenzo in reply asked which head he wished. "If this is the case," the Pope remarked, "you know how to do everything," and ordered him to sketch a St. Paul. This he did to perfection with free bold strokes in a half an hour to the keen delight and marvel of the Pope. Paul V was very anxious that the genius of Giovan Lorenzo, still young and tender, be sustained by an authoritative hand and stimulated to reach that degree of eminence that the prognosticators promised. Therefore, he entrusted Bernini to Cardinal Maffeo Barberini, a great devotee and patron of the noblest arts, who fortunately happened to be present. He strictly enjoined the Cardinal not only to attend with every care to Bernini's studies but also to give them fire and enthusiasm. He told him that he stood as the guarantor of the brilliant result that was expected of Bernini. And then the Pope, after encouraging the boy with kind words to continue the career he had begun with good heart, gave him twelve gold medals, which were as many as he could hold in his hands, and turning to the Cardinal, said prophetically, "We hope that this youth will become the Michelangelo of his century."

The boy, instead of vainly inflating himself because of the success of his efforts and the praise of the mighty (a practice befitting only the small-minded and those whose goal is all things save the attainment of true glory), tirelessly dedicated himself to new and continuous study. But what cannot a gifted nature accomplish when it is accompanied by wise and prudent guidance! His father, to whom he showed his fine studies, expressed both admiration and disparagement, praising the drawings while telling him that he was sure that he could not achieve the same result a second time, as if to say that the perfection of the first efforts was due to a lucky accident, rather than to his son's ability. This was a very clever device as each day Giovan Lorenzo attempted to emulate his own virtues, and thus he was in constant competition with himself. It is not surprising, therefore, that from that time onward Bernini was always filled with such zeal and desire to always do better that when he was old he confessed that he had never done anything that completely pleased him if he compared it with whatever he had later worked on or, at least, in reference to that which, according to new ideas he had conceived, he would have wanted to do.

During this period the boy Bernini was so enamoured of art that not only were his innermost thoughts bound to it, but his greatest joy was to be with the most celebrated artists. It happened one day that he found himself in the company of Annibale Carracci and other masters in the basilica of St. Peter's. They had finished their devotions and were leaving the church when that great master, turning toward the tribune, said, "Believe me, the day will come, when, no one knows, that a prodigious genius will make two great monuments in the middle and at the end of this temple on a scale in keeping with the vastness of the building." That was enough to set Bernini afire with desire to execute them himself and, not being able to restrain his inner impulse, he said in heartfelt words, "Oh, if only I could be the one." Thus, unconsciously, he interpreted Annibale's prophecy and later brought it to pass, as we will relate in due course when we tell of the wonderful works he executed for those places.

Not much later Jacopo Foys Montoia decided to order his tomb with his own portrait carved in marble for the Church of S. Jacopo degli Spagnuoli. He gave the commission to the youthful artist. Bernini made a portrait of him so very lifelike that in our time there was no one who was not stunned by it. When the work had been put in place many cardinals and other prelates came to the church for the express purpose of seeing such a fine work. One of them said, "This is Montoia petrified." The words were scarcely out of his mouth when Montoia himself appeared. Cardinal Maffeo Barberini, later to be Urban VIII, who was also among the cardinals, went to meet him and touching him said, "This is the portrait of Monsignor Montoia," and turning to the statue, "and this is Monsignor Montoia."

After that work Bernini carved the bust of Cardinal Bellarmino which was placed over his venerated tomb. Next to the bust he sculpted the figure representing Religion.

His Holiness, Pope Paul V, also wished to have his portrait made by Bernini. Afterward, the artist carved the portrait of Cardinal Scipione Borghese, the Pope's nephew. This handsome work was almost completed when a mishap occurred. A crack appeared in the marble across the whole of the forehead. Bernini, who was very bold and who already had a marvelous knowledge of the working of marble, in order to free himself, and even more the Cardinal, from the embarrassment resulting from bringing such news to him, had a sufficiently large piece of marble of known quality secretly brought to him. Without telling a soul, he worked for fifteen nights (which was all the time he had for that tedious task) on another bust exactly like the first and not one jot less in beauty. He then had the first bust transported to his studio, well wrapped, so that no one in his household would be able to see it. Then he waited for the Cardinal to come to see the completed work. That gentleman finally arrived and saw the first portrait, whose defect in the polished state appeared even more prominent and disfiguring. At first glance the Cardinal became agitated, but he masked it in order not to distress Bernini. The astute artist, meanwhile, pretended to be unaware of the Cardinal's disappointment, and since relief is more satisfying when the suffering has been most severe, he engaged the Cardinal in conversation before finally uncovering the other beautiful portrait. The gaiety that the prelate displayed upon seeing the second portrait without defect made very evident how much pain he had felt when he beheld the first one. The diligent care that Bernini employed to avoid offending him pleased the Cardinal so much that from that day onward he loved him tenderly. Today both portraits are to be found in the Palace of Villa Borghese. They are such fine and splendid works that Bernini himself, when coming upon them with Cardinal Antonio Barberini forty years later, exclaimed, "How little progress I have made in the art of sculpture through these long years becomes clear to me when I see that as a boy I handled marble in this manner."

Meanwhile, still in his fifteenth year, he carved the figure of St. Lawrence on the gridiron for Leone Strozzi, which was placed in the Strozzi villa. Then, for the previously mentioned Cardinal Borghese, he made the group of Aeneas carrying the aged Anchises, figures rather more than life-size. This was his first large work. In it, although something of the manner of his father, Pietro, is discernible, one still can see, through the fine touches in the execution, a certain approach to the tender and true toward which from then on his excellent taste led him. It appears most clearly in the head of the old man.

It is not surprising that this same cardinal immediately commissioned him to do a statue of David of equal size. In this work Bernini overwhelmingly surpassed himself. He completed it within a period of no more than seven months, thanks to the fact that from youth, as he was wont to say, he devoured marble and never struck a false blow, an accomplishment of those who have made themselves superior to art itself rather than of those who are merely expert in art. He modeled the beautiful face of this figure after his own countenance. The powerful knitted brows, the terrible fixity of the eyes, and the upper jaw clamped tightly over the lower lip wonderfully express the rightful wrath of the young Israelite in the act of aiming his sling at the forehead of the giant Philistine. The same spirit of resoluteness and vigor is seen in all parts of the body, which lacks only movement to be alive. It is worth recording that while Bernini was working on the figure in his own likeness, Cardinal Maffeo Barberini came often to his studio and held the mirror for him with his own hand.

But Cardinal Borghese, to whom it seemed that it was by chance—as indeed it was—that he had discovered a treasure in this great creator, would not permit him to remain in his service without some beautiful work underway, so he had him carve the group of the youthful Apollo with Daphne who is in the process of changing into a laurel tree. My wish here to describe the marvels that all eyes find in this great work is futile, since only the eye and not the ear can form an adequate impression of it. In its design, in the proportions, in the expression of the heads, in the exquisiteness of all the parts, and in the fineness of its workmanship it surpasses anything imaginable. In the eyes of the expert and learned, Bernini's Daphne always was and always will be a miracle of art, since it is in itself the standard of excellence. I need only say that as soon as it was finished such acclamation arose that all Rome rushed to view it as though it were a miracle. When he walked about the city, the young artist, who had not yet attained his nineteenth year, attracted everyone's eye. People watched him and pointed him out to others as a prodigy. Certainly, from that time onward everyone who came to Rome and wished to see splendid things had among his chief objectives that of viewing a work of such magnificence. In order that the figure of Daphne—so true and alive—would be less offensive to the eyes of a chaste spectator, Cardinal Maffeo Barberini had carved there the following distich, the noble fruit of his most erudite mind:

The lover who will fleeting beauty follow
Plucks bitter berries; leaves fill his hand's hollow.

Meanwhile, Pope Paul V died and the holy tiara was given to Alessandro Cardinal Ludovisi of the most noble Bolognese family, who took the name Gregory XV. Not much time elapsed before the new Pope, who appreciated Bernini's merit above that of any other artist of his age, was pleased to engage him to carve his portrait. Bernini made not one portrait but three, in both marble and bronze. The portraits corresponded so much to the pontiff's expectations that Bernini gained a great measure of esteem through them. Afterwards, the cardinal-nephew, knowing that Bernini possessed great nobility of thought and not a little erudition to match his excellence in art, was pleased to have him dine with him regularly on holidays in order that he might engage him in stimulating conversation. He arranged for Bernini to receive the Order of Christ and the rich pension that went with it. During this period Cardinal Borghese presented to Cardinal Ludovico Ludovisi the beautiful group of the Rape of Proserpine which Bernini had carved for him shortly before. Cardinal Ludovisi rewarded the artist no less generously for it than if it had been made expressly for him. There is no doubt that if the reign of Gregory XV had been less brief Giovan Lorenzo would have been commissioned to do great and most honorable works such as he later executed for his illustrious successors. Before he assumed the papacy with the name of Urban VIII, Cardinal Maffeo Barberini had been a colleague of Gregory XV in the Apostolic Chamber. He now became his fortunate successor in that highest of offices.

A vast range of opportunities opened for Bernini upon Urban's succession. Scarcely had this great pontiff ascended the sacred throne when he had Bernini brought to him. Receiving him affectionately, he spoke to him thus: "It is your great fortune, Cavalier, to see Cardinal Maffeo Barberini Pope, but our fortune is far greater in that Cavalier Bernini lives during our pontificate." The Pope had Bernini make many portraits of his person in marble and bronze, and as time went on Bernini made still more. From the time that His Holiness Paul V had entrusted him with this noble genius, Urban VIII had foreseen great things of Bernini. The Pope had conceived the lofty ambition that in his pontificate Rome would produce another Michelangelo. His ambition grew even stronger, as he already had in mind the magnificent idea for the high altar of St. Peter's in the area which we call the confession and also for the painting of the benediction loggia. Therefore, the Pope informed Bernini that it was his wish that he dedicate a large part of his time to the study of architecture and painting so that he could unite with distinction these disciplines to his other virtues. The youth did not hesitate in agreeing with the counsel of his friend, the pontiff.

He studied under no masters other than the antique statues and buildings of Rome, which were as numerous, he used to say, in the city as masters whose instruction had to be paid for by youthful artists. For a period of two continuous years he devoted himself to painting; that is, to gaining experience in handling color, since he had already mastered the great problems of drawing through intensive study. During this period, without neglecting the study of architecture, he painted a great number of pictures both large and small which today display their splendid qualities in Rome's most celebrated galleries and in other worthy places. We will speak of these in detail elsewhere. Later the Pope wished to put in operation his grand concept of the decoration of the confession of SS. Peter and Paul in the Vatican basilica which we mentioned earlier. He gave the commission to Bernini, allotting him three hundred scudi monthly for this purpose.

It seems that my task would now be the description of the great work he hastened to execute: the four marvelous metal columns which hold up the baldachin together with its beautiful crowning element surmounted by the cross. But I think I may be excused from describing it, as well as the other works by his hand or after his design that are exposed to the admiration of the public in this church. If there should be anyone who would like to know why, I hasten to make it clear. The nobility, the vastness, and all the marvels of this great temple have been described with uncommon accuracy by many in the past and by many more and better in the present century. Others have enabled them to be seen and enjoyed even in distant lands through prints made of them. Nevertheless, I never knew anyone, myself included, who on going there in person to see with his own eyes did not find them much superior to the idea that he had earlier conceived of them. What appears to the viewer is something completely new, something he had never dreamed of seeing. From this I draw the conclusion that for the eye alone and not the ear is reserved the merit of being able to render a complete judgment. Indeed, I will go even further and say that the eye itself at first sight is not capable of conveying it all to the imagination, such is the abundance of sublime ornament offered at one time to the eye. A very clear indication of this is that there is no one, no matter how judicious or expert he may be, whose spirit is sufficiently satisfied by the first sight to form any concept other than that of complete wonderment. One must, therefore, come and come again, see and resee, and always that lofty temple is rediscovered in its whole and in its every major part. I would thus count the time completely wasted that I might spend in such a description. I will only say that scarcely had Bernini's great concept become known and had begun to take form in the immense columns, when inexperienced and stupid people started the same sort of whispering campaign against him that had been raised against the great Brunelleschi by the ignorant lowlife of Florence: that Brunelleschi had prepared so much marble for building the great dome that it seemed to be enough to build a city. Finally Brunelleschi proved to them that just so much and no less marble would be necessary to carry to perfection that marvel of the world. So the tongues of the fools wagged, with everyone wanting to give his opinion. Their conclusion was that, as projected, Bernini's work would undoubtedly fill that great temple and occupy the best part of it. But they were disappointed, since quite the contrary was found to be true when it was finished.

Bernini completed this stupendous work in the space of nine years. The Pope wished to compensate the creator, but it seemed well to hear the judgment and opinion of various persons concerning the great work first. A group was assembled for this purpose. Many said many things; one person was of the opinion that it would be appropriate to give Bernini a gold chain worth five hundred ducats. When this idea was repeated to the Pope he immediately said, smiling, "Well now, the gold will be Bernini's, but the chain is due the one who gave such fine advice." The Pope had ten thousand scudi and certain pensions given Bernini. He gave a canonry of St. John Lateran and a benefice of St. Peter's to two of Bernini's brothers. These were words and actions truly worthy of the monarch that he was. Bernini used to say it was by chance that his work came out so well, implying that under such a great dome and in such a vast space and among such massive piers, artistic skill alone could never arrive at suitable dimensions and proportions, although, on the contrary, the artist's genius and mind could envisage the appropriate dimensions without the help of any rules.

At this juncture I can no longer remain silent regarding the fountain that Bernini executed in Piazza di Spagna at the instigation of the same pontiff, Urban VIII, since in it his genius as usual shines forth. In this location the low pressure of the water did not permit it to spout much above the level of the land, so that any effect of richness or magnificence would be difficult to achieve. Bernini, therefore, constructed a large and beautiful basin to be filled with water from the fountain. In the middle of the basin, almost as if it were rising and falling in the midst of the sea, he placed a fine graceful ship. From several parts of the ship water gushed forth abundantly, as if from so many cannons. This concept seemed so beautiful to the Pope that he did not scorn illustrating it with the following beautiful lines:

The papal war machines shoot forth not flames
But waters sweet that quench the fires of war.

But in the literary world there is never a shortage of confused minds, quick to envy the glory of others and always willing to think the worst of everyone, and in thinking it to believe it, and in believing it to publish it—something more monstrous than savage. The following distich, in response to the Pope's very sensitive lines, was attached to the fountain itself and circulated outside Rome:

The Urban Poet has made a fountain of poems,
Not poems of a fountain; thus poets please themselves.

With that distich the indiscreet poet tried to diminish the wonderful animation of that lofty genius, the noble ideas and the always distinguished restraint and, at the same time, to attribute to others the glory due Bernini for such extraordinary originality. I wish to make plain to the world, in noting such a thing here, that sometimes the cloud of envy reaches even the loftiest stars.

But since we are speaking of fountains, I shall say that it was always Bernini's opinion that in designing fountains the good architect had to give them some real significance or, at least, an allusion to something noble, whether real or imagined. While Pope Urban VIII was still alive, Bernini put this principle into practice in the beautiful fountain in Piazza Barberini which was made from his design and by his chisel. He carved three dolphins which hold up the basin, above which is the beautiful figure of Glaucas sounding his conch shell from which water gushes.

At the instigation of Urban VIII, Bernini adorned, after his own designs, the four great niches in the piers which carry the great dome of St. Peter's. These niches are below the relics. Earlier, an iron grating covered the space from top to bottom. These niches, then, were the admirable receptacles for four colossi of marble made by four highly individual artists. Longinus is from the chisel of Giovan Lorenzo Bernini; St. Andrew is the work of Francesco Fiammingo; St. Helena was carved by Andrea Bolgi; and Veronica is the beautiful work of Francesco Mochi.

The Pope restored the ancient church of S. Bibiana situated in the celebrated place called *ad ursum pileatum,* a catacomb very rich in treasures of martyred saints. During the restoration it pleased God that as a reward for such pious action the body of that saint should be recovered. So great and universal was the joy in Rome for the glad news that Bernini was ordered to make a statue of the saint which was then placed in the church in the place where it is now seen. Nor, while on the subject, do I wish to leave unsaid that on this occasion an ancient and badly composed marble figure of a bear wearing a hat was also found. It is precisely that figure which is today on the wall in the small piazza of the church.

The Pope, whose opinion of Bernini and his future grew greater every day, desired to make him, so to speak, immortal. He never stopped trying to persuade him to marry, not so much that some child and heir to his virtue be left to Rome, but in order that he might have someone to look after him so that he might have more time and peace for his art. Although the Cavalier showed repugnance at the suggestion, saying that the statues he carved would be his children and that they would keep his memory alive in the world for many centuries, in the end he decided to give way to the Pope's counsel and to accommodate himself to the married state. During the course of the year of 1639 he chose, among the fine offers made to him, the daughter of Paolo Tezio, secretary of the SS. Nunziata, a man of great worth and goodness. He lived with his wife thirty-three years and many children were born of the union.

But to return to where we left off: the works that Bernini executed during the life of Urban VIII were so many that in order not to bore the reader we will deal with them briefly and without regard to chronological order. He made the design for Palazzo Barberini, for the campanile of St. Peter's, and for the facade of the Collegio de Propaganda Fide, which was threatening to crash down. He reinforced it with such skillful artistry that even the ornament serves as a buttress to the building. No one not well informed of the real facts would ever guess it. He sculpted the bas-relief set over the main door of St. Peter's. In it one sees the figure of Christ who, speaking to the Prince of the Apostles, says: *Pasce oves meas.*

He also made the design and model for the tomb of the Countess Matilda. In spite of what has been written by another author, his disciple, Stefano Speranza, carved only the bas-relief; the putto over the sarcophagus is by Andrea Bolgi. The putto on the right is by Luigi Bernini, who also made the statue of the Countess, except for the head which was done entirely by Cavalier Giovan Lorenzo. The two putti with the coat of arms were made by

Matteo Buonarelli, another of Bernini's pupils and husband of that Costanza whose portrait, in a head with a small bust made by Bernini, is seen in the Royal Gallery of the Most Serene Grand Duke. It is quite true, however, that in all these works, besides the model and design, Bernini always did some retouching with his own hand.

He also carved the statue of Urban VIII which was placed in the Capitoline, as well as many other portraits of the Pope and the Barberini family.

But what shall we say of that great miracle of art, the grand tomb of Urban VIII that Bernini made in marble and bronze for St. Peter's. This monument, truly, has in it qualities so original that if anyone came to Rome solely to see it, he could be sure of expending well his time, effort, and his expense. It stands in an immense niche on the left of the great chapel of the cathedra. Between two columns of smooth marble an oblong base or block rises from the floor, repeated three times, that is to say, in three registers. Above it stands the tomb's great sarcophagus, richly ornamented. Above the sarcophagus rises a great plinth which supports the large bronze statue of Urban VIII, enthroned, and in the act of benediction. He is so realistically described that nothing more could be desired. On the left Justice is represented, with two infants beside her, one and one-half times life-size in the finest, whitest marble. Leaning against the sarcophagus, she raises her eyes to the figure of the pontiff, and seems immersed in the most profound sorrow. Charity is on the left. She has a suckling infant at her breast and another larger child beside her who looks upward, unrestrainedly grieving at the loss of that great father, while Charity looks at him with compassion. She seems to be giving testimony of her own sorrow by expressing her grief at the child's tears. Over the great sarcophagus in the very center of the composition, we see the figure of Death. She is at once shameful and proud. Her back is winged and turned away from us; her head is partially veiled and covered, with the face turned inward.

The large book in her hand is poetically imagined to be the one used by Death to register the names of the popes cut down by her scythe. She appears in the act of writing in letters of gold the words: URBANUS VIII. BARBERINUS PONT. MAX.

On that tiny section of the preceding page that Bernini's skillful artistry makes visible, we see written in letters of gold a part of the name of Gregory, Urban's predecessor. Truly a completely magnificent concept, the tomb was the admiration of all and gave occasion for the lofty talent of Cardinal Rapaccioli, who composed in the artist's praise the following spirited lines:

So living has Bernini made great Urban,
His spirit so impressed into hard bronze,
That to restore belief here Death herself
Stands on the sepulchre to prove him dead.

This stupendous work was begun two years before Urban's death and unveiled about thirty months after he went to Heaven in the presence of Pope Innocent X, his successor. I do not wish to neglect reporting here a sharp response that Bernini made to a person of high rank, unfriendly to the house of Barberini, who was looking at the tomb with some other people. Through a certain whimsy Bernini had placed here and there over the tomb some bees, which allude to the Pope's coat of arms. That personage observed them and said, "Signor Cavaliere, Your Lordship must have wished to show the dispersion of the Barberini family by the random placing of these bees" (for at that time members of the house were in retirement in France). Bernini replied, "Your Lordship, however, knows well that dispersed bees congregate at the sound of a bell," referring to the great bell of the Capitoline which sounds after the death of a pope.

The fame of the artist became ever more widespread throughout the world. With every day his name became brighter. Therefore, it is not surprising that the greatest rulers of Europe began to compete with one another to gain possession of his works. Charles I, the unhappy King of England, wanted to have his portrait done by Bernini's chisel. After gently importuning him he had sent from London to the artist the fine painting by Anthony Van Dyck. I saw this painting less than two months ago in the house of Bernini's two sons. In the painting we see the King portrayed from life in three poses, that is to say, in three views: full face, left profile and right profile. Bernini, after first obtaining the permission of the Pope, executed the portrait with his customary admirable skill. He sent it to King Charles in the care of a certain Bonifazio, his apprentice. After happily accepting it, the King took from his finger a diamond valued at six thousand scudi and, handing it to the Cavalier's envoy, said: "Adorn that hand which made so fine a work." Moreover, he sent Bernini precious gifts of beautiful cloths and other delights of his country. To Bernini's envoy the King gave a gratuity of one thousand scudi. The work so pleased Her Highness the Queen that she had a great desire to have one of herself done also by the same hand. She, therefore, wrote Bernini the following letter:

Signor Cavaliere Bernini,

The esteem that the King, my Lord, and I have for the statue that you made of him is accompanied by the satisfaction that we have in it as a work that merits the approbation of all who look upon it and compells me now to tell you that in order to make my satisfaction complete I would like a similar one of myself made by your hand from portraits that will be given you by Signor Lomes, on whom I rely to assure you more particularly of the gratitude that I shall hold for the pleasure I expect of you on this occasion. I pray God will keep you in His holy care.

Given in Whitehall, 26 June 1639.

Henrietta Maria, R.

However, the turbulence that broke out a little later in that kingdom prevented the execution of the portrait. It is, however, true that a very noble and rich cavalier of London, after seeing the King's bust among others, was so aflame with desire to have his own portrait done that he decided to go to Rome for that purpose. To a friend who asked him what assurance he had of getting a portrait before undertaking such a long pilgrimage since (as he said) Bernini did not work at the importunities of anyone who asked him but only for those who most pleased him, he replied, "I will compensate him as the King has done and not less." So he came to Rome and returned to his country with his portrait, after having given Cavalier Bernini six thousand scudi.

Cardinal de Richelieu never ceased urging in his letters from France to Cardinal Antonio Barberini that he induce the artist to make his portrait. Bernini gave in to these importunities. When the work was finished he sent it, along with a letter, in the charge of Jacopo Balsimelli, then in his service, so that both could be given to Cardinal de Richelieu. To give the episode greater clarity I am pleased to quote the letter here:

Most Eminent, Reverend, and Venerable Lord Patron,

The Most Eminent Cardinal Antonio, my Lord, with extraordinary solicitude wished that I engage myself in carving a statue of Your Eminence. His authority found my spirit already most disposed by the ambition I have always had of demonstrating my homage for the sublime grandeur of Your Eminence. It would never appear to me that I was of any value in this century if I should fail to serve that person who has so illuminated it. The impatience that I had to begin and to assure myself of this glory has hastened the present portrait, so that if Your Eminence considers this little work of mine worthy of your chamber you will have near at hand something that constantly recalls my devotion. In extenuation of its shortcomings I must implore you to deign to give some thought to the disadvantage of the distance. If, indeed, I have been successful in serving you, know that God Almighty, whose favor you compel by your virtue, has assisted me. Permit me the grace of continuing to call myself,

From Rome

Your Most Humble and Devoted Servant
Giovan Lorenzo Bernino

That magnanimous prince, to whom the work greatly appealed, sent our artist a jewel made of diamonds. I do not know its value, but the fact that Balsimelli was given eight hundred scudi for nothing more than presenting the portrait in Bernini's name is a most cogent indication of the Cardinal's great esteem. In confirmation of my conjecture I shall now take the liberty of including another letter that Bernini wrote to the Cardinal to thank him for such a generous gift:

Most Eminent, Reverend and Venerable Lord Patron,

I do not know how to thank Your Eminence for the most precious gift you were pleased to send me. Being aware of my small merit, I was fearful of offending with my work your grandeur which functions in relation to itself alone. But for my own sake I must splendidly proclaim to one and all such a precious manifestation of your favor, so that there may perhaps be attributed to the portrait I carved of Your Eminence the value it acquired through its remuneration—credit that the creator's hand cannot bestow on it. Much more than any other joy I esteem the praises that I receive from that person who is now the sole object of all panegyrics. Even though I know that I am unworthy, yet I do not dare to be alone in this century in opposing the most subtle judgment of Your Eminence. Nor can I do other than believe that the bust is satisfactory, since Signor Cardinal Mazzarini has indicated to me that Your Eminence wishes me to have the honorable task of executing the entire statue. I have clearly in mind the order concerning it given me by Cardinal Antonio. I gladly accept the reminders that Signor Cardinal Mazzarini now presses upon me. Most powerful always will be the spur to my ambition to have the recognition

Of Your Most Reverend Eminence,
Rome, 24 May 1642

Your Most Humble and Devoted Servant
Giovan Lorenzo Bernini

In the course of the year of 1644, the last year of the pontificate of Urban VIII, His Majesty the King of France, Louis XIII of noble memory, ordered Cardinal Mazzarini, with whom the Cavalier was very friendly in Rome, to write to Bernini in the King's name to come to France to live with the promise of an annual stipend of twelve thousand scudi. This great man might perhaps have been lost to Italy because of the request, if Bernini, always mindful of the kindnesses of Urban VIII, had not left the decision to him. Urban decided that Bernini should refuse, because as the Pope told him (almost prophetically), he was made for Rome and Rome was made for him. All the letters in which

Mazzarini urged, on the King's orders, that Bernini come to France have not come into our hands. However, the one which I will quote very clearly indicates that after July of 1644, when Urban died, negotiations were resumed. Without doubt Bernini would have been inclined to go into the service of that monarch, if it had not been for his grateful memory of the person of that pontiff, to whom Rome owes the retention within its walls of such a rare man. Here is the letter:

Most Illustrious Signore,

If doubt of my constant desire for your services might have offended Your Lordship, I wish to believe that you will be willing to excuse my tardiness in sending you the enclosed brevets because of my continual heavy duties. I have ordered my envoy Benedetti to accompany them with warm expressions of affection and esteem and to assure you that everywhere and always I will espouse with particular enthusiasm every occasion for your greater profit and glory. This Your Lordship will have an opportunity to discover when you are here in the Service of His Majesty where, in brief, the aspect is in conformity with the hopes that you put forward on the 19th past, which was reported to me by my agent, who will convey by word of mouth my wishes finally for your true happiness. Paris, etc.

Affectionately from the heart
Cardinal Mazzarini

But since we have now come to the last days of Urban VIII, we would like, before going on with our chronicle, to give briefly some further indication of the marked love with which Bernini was always treated by that pontiff. First of all the Pope wished that Bernini treat him always with the same intimacy as when he was a cardinal. The Pope as a normal practice gave Bernini free access to his private quarters without a prior appointment. During the dinner hour the Pope used to have pleasant conversation with him till it was time to retire. When sleep brought an end to discussion, it was Bernini's task to pull the blinds, close the windows, and take his leave. As a consequence of the Pope's love and esteem and in order to compensate him handsomely on all occasions, Bernini was made the architect of St. Peter's. But since he well knew that no incentive is more efficacious than honor—the sole reward of virtue—to inspire noble souls to ascend to always more worthy tasks, he sought at all times to honor him in every way. Nor do I wish to leave this subject without noting a remarkable instance, which because of the surrounding circumstances is quite exemplary. One day the Pope called in Paolo Allaleona, his chief master of ceremonies, and said to him, "Paolo, we would like to go in person today to Bernini's house to refresh ourselves somewhat with the sight of his works. What do you think?" "Holy Father," replied Paolo, "it would seem to me that such a visit by Your Holiness would be taxing and I would not advise it." At this the Pope replied, "Well then, we will go to our nephew's house and amuse ourselves with the children." "Oh yes, that I should like," said the master of ceremonies. "You really are an ignoramus," responded the Pope, "not to realize that for us to go in person to see the children would be puerile, whereas to render honor of this sort to the home of a virtuoso of such caliber would be an act of magnanimity in which virtue would be both honored and increased in him and in others." And that very day, accompanied by sixteen cardinals, the Pope went to Bernini's house, to the marvel and applause of all Rome.

The trust and love shown by Urban to our artist was equalled by his nephews, Francesco and, particularly, Antonio, who, in addition to bestowing on him high and most noble public tributes, arranged for a pension of five hundred scudi a year to be given to

Bernini's son, Abbot Pier Filippo, who today is a worthy prelate of the Roman Court. In addition to his most affable nature and his great talent for heroic poetry, he marvelously joined to them the study of literature. He is recognized as the worthy heir to the sublime talents of such a father.

At the urging and expense of Cardinal Antonio Barberini, Bernini composed and produced—with the help of other artists; that is to say, of painters, sculptors and architects—fine edifying plays of which we shall speak at the opportune time, when we shall discuss these and other plays that were admired in Rome—plays in which marvelous stage machinery, the fruit of Bernini's genius and financed by Cardinal Antonio himself, was utilized.

Such high merit accompanied by the great unwavering good fortune enjoyed by Bernini during the long pontificate of Urban VIII—qualities rarely if ever seen joined in the same person—could not, during the lifetime and after the death of Urban VIII, help inciting in the hearts of those jealous of Bernini glowing sparks of rancor and disdain. The sparks spread and settled in those spirits most receptive and predisposed to the injury of Bernini. These sparks could not but be converted into a great fire capable of consuming not only Bernini's past fortune but also, in great part, that glory which he had gained over so long a period by his most laudable accomplishments, as we are now about to relate.

First, though, it would be useful to point out the misfortunes that served as foundations for those who wished Bernini ill and for their sinister intentions or, to be more precise, that served as a pretext to employ every unseemly trick against him. His Holiness Urban VIII had the interior of St. Peter's embellished. He had placed in the center of the church, under the dome, the marvelous bronze altar with four columns. He also had the decoration of the four niches completed by the addition of marble bas-reliefs, pilasters, columns in various stones, and balustrades. In addition, he completed the other four niches in the piers beneath the dome at the ground level of the church. The Pope then decided to decorate the outside of the church as well. He wished to complete the two bell towers on either side of the facade. The bell towers had been started under Paul V, but they had been constructed only up to the level of the balustrade which crowns the top of the facade proper. As usual, the Pope gave the commission to Bernini. Bernini not only made the design for it but also a fine model which gained the approval of that learned pontiff and the applause of the very eminent cardinals who were members of the Congregation of the Fabbrica of St. Peter's. Therefore, they asked him to start work at once. It was the Pope's custom, whenever buildings were to be erected in places where foundations of other buildings might exist, to take necessary precautions in order to ascertain if, in fact, there were any such foundations. He therefore, issued a specific order to the Congregation to call in two of the best master builders then in the city of Rome, who, since the time of Paul, had been employed in laying foundations.

They were Giovanni Colarmeno and Pietro Paolo (last name unknown). They attested to the complete soundness and stability of the foundations so positively that the Pope and the Congregation were satisfied that it would be well to give new orders to Bernini to continue the construction of the bell towers, and a decree was issued to this effect. Thus the prudent artist had reason to turn to the enterprise with security, not to mention the probability of the great honor that the work would bring him. The first bell tower on which he worked was on the right side of the facade toward the Holy Office.

It was formed of two orders of columns and pilasters, the first order being Corinthian. Its height from the top of its base, which was on a line with the top of the balustrade, to its cornice was seventy-two Roman palmi. The second order was made up of a base fourteen palmi high, and in the middle of the archway opening ran a balustrade with its socle, base, and coping. Above it the pedestal, the columns, and the pilasters were gracefully set.

Altogether—base, column, capital, architrave, frieze, and cornice—it rose to a height of forty-six and a half palmi. Finally, there was a third or attic story, forty-five palmi in height, formed of pilasters and two columns on either side of the open archway in the center. All in all, as is easy to see from the wooden model still in the office of the Fabbrica, the three orders reached a height of one hundred and seventy-seven and a half palmi. All of these plans were put in operation. For the time being, the pyramid that was to serve as a finial for the tower was made of wood so that the whole structure could be seen in place. The pyramidal finial was to be made of the same stone as the other three orders. Since it was to be of an irregular shape and not perfectly square, it would be made of stone carved to the proper measure. When everything was done, it happened that the central facade between the two bell towers was affected in some parts. Cracks appeared in exactly those places where in the time of Paul V the vault of the porch had been built in front of the church. The cracks appeared in the gilded stucco ornaments under that vault. Those opposed to Bernini quickly took up arms and said more against him than ever before. They reiterated constantly that the bell tower had shifted its position and that this had caused the cracks in the vault as well as in the outer facade. They said that these were the ruinous results visited on Rome by those popes who were pleased to give all the work to one man alone, although there was an abundance of meritorious men in the city. They said it was as if Rome, rich throughout the ages in sublime artists, had become a denuded and sterile field. By these and similar statements, about which it is better to remain silent than to discuss, they endeavored to influence the Pope. These whisperings against Bernini would have had little effect if Urban VIII had not died at just the time when they were going on, while the bell tower was still unfinished.

When Innocent X was elevated to that supreme office, a vast field of intrigue opened up against Bernini with little regard for the memory of Urban VIII. People whom Pope Innocent X trusted and who, though he thought them very experienced, were on the contrary little informed concerning these arts, were made use of. They, thus, knew well what to say and do to make the Pope believe that Urban VIII and Bernini did great damage to that most noble facade with the newly constructed bell towers, and that one of these towers, now almost completed, was by its great weight bringing about inevitable ruin. One of the first ill effects of these lies was that the Pope was persuaded to use another person to build his family palace as well as the churches of St. John Lateran and S. Agnese in Piazza Navona. Later, the Pope wished to see Bernini and to question him regarding matters of which he had already been convinced. The Cavalier responded that he had built over the foundations laid by Carlo Maderno, and that this alone would have been sufficient for him to believe in all prudence that he could work with security. But even so he had not wanted to start work without diligent efforts to establish the state of stability and soundness of the foundations. The decree of the Congregation of the Fabbrica regarding it followed. Lastly, they received, because of his judgment, the certification of two master builders who had been in charge of such work since the time of Paul V. In addition, Bernini said that it was his opinion that the movement of the facade was caused by the settling of the bell tower: a usual thing in any building of extraordinary size. It was apparent that his bell tower was entirely in plumb, as he had made a test and there was no lean on any of the four sides. Nor could it be otherwise, since it was built in accordance with good architectural principles. Bernini said that if it pleased His Holiness, he would have two trial shafts sunk so that, conjectures laid aside, the Pope could see underneath with his own eyes whether there was any cause there for such movement. Such a very judicious proposal could not but be pleasing to the Pope. Therefore, he quickly gave an order to have two shafts made—one inside on a plumb line with the point where the movement was seen, and the other in front of the facade. By means of these shafts, Bernini, together with the other architects assigned to the project, confirmed the source of the trouble, and an account of it was given to the pontiff. The Pope formed a special committee to convene in his presence, and thus he could listen at length to the various opinions of the architects. The opinion of those most qualified was that the bell tower was in no danger of collapse but was properly settling itself. They also said that such settling was taking place because Carlo Maderno, the architect who erected the facade in the time of Paul V, in order to strengthen the facade (one side of which, toward the Holy Office, is incorrectly laid out since its foundations are not in alignment with the longitudinal axis of the church), made the two bell towers and raised them up to the top of the facade, so that the center facade was firmly held and buttressed. In building the bell tower on the side toward the Holy Office, a mistake was made in excavating the foundations, that is, they excavated below the foundations of the facade, so that the ground fell away or, as we say, slipped. A great deal of earth under the facade crumbled and there was soon a considerable movement in the central section. Maderno, considering the imminent danger of the collapse of that great edifice because of this unforeseen misfortune, had sixteen shafts sunk in the stretch of crumbling earth. These he had filled with stones immersed in lime. Over these filled shafts he laid the foundations for the bell tower. Since Bernini was unable to take all the measures that such an operation called for because of the fear that arose about the immediate peril to the facade, it is not surprising that the facade had in some places yielded to the weight of the bell tower which was now increased by the addition of the two stories plus the attic story. These reasons convinced the pontiff. He said it seemed a good idea to him that the weight of the bell tower should be lightened by removing the attic story and that then the foundations could be strengthened. Here my reader should note that everything I have related is dealt with in written documents contained in the archives of the Fabbrica.

The plan pleased the experts and Bernini was already

thinking of starting the work when it chanced that the pontiff went to one of his estates called S. Martino, not far from Viterbo, for repose. While he was there enemies of Bernini and the Barberini family, especially a certain person semiskilled in art whom the Pope greatly trusted, were also present. They knew how to use such opportunities to persuade the Pope by intensive arguments. The Pope finally issued a command that not only the attic story but also the other stories erected by Bernini be demolished.

The Pope's order was quickly executed (perhaps so that Bernini could do nothing about it) to the sorrow of the whole city. The dismantling of such a beautiful work, one that had become known to everyone, caused still greater distress with the knowledge that it could have been safeguarded from that danger more imagined than real. It was the opinion of many that this war against Bernini was waged not so much because of dislike of the artist personally and of the memory of Urban VIII as because of the desire that, when it happened that the Pope for some reason would become displeased with Bernini, he would then appoint Borromini to succeed him in the office of architect of St. Peter's. Borromini had been Bernini's disciple but, in truth, had little gratitude toward him. He was present at the conferences I mentioned previously and although others opposed Bernini, he alone stated his opposition without esteem or respect. He alone inveighed against Bernini with his whole heart and soul.

In order not to go on too long, I will say finally that according to an authoritative source, the Pope in speaking of his confidant—that certain minister with little artistic competence—said one day that he had been rushed into making three decisions by him, one of which was the demolition of the bell tower of St. Peter's.

But when a man loses that which he is accustomed to having, or if he does not have that which he desires, he often gives way to his feelings, and like a city assailed by enemies his peace is destroyed, and he is kept in continual torment to a degree commensurate with his longings. They are deemed the wisest, therefore, who least allow themselves to be carried away by such passion. That a man such as Bernini be subjected to the ordeal of persecutions and lose for a short time the acclaim that his genius attracted from every quarter was necessary in order that the world might have knowledge of the steadfastness of his powers and other gifts of his spirit, gifts which gained greater magnificence not only through the resoluteness with which he endured many blows but also through his absolute command of his emotions. Thus he lived tranquilly and carried his work on with great diligence. During this very period he brought forth for Rome to see the most beautiful works he had ever done.

Chief among these were the design for the chapel of Cardinal Federigo Cornaro in the church of the Discalced Carmelites, S. Maria della Vittoria, which stands not far from the Porta Pia, and the wonderful group of St. Theresa and the Angel who pierces the Saint's heart with the arrow of Divine Love while she is in the transports of the sweetest ecstasy. For its great tenderness and for all its other qualities this work has always been an object of admiration. I shall not attempt to praise it at length. It is enough to relate that Bernini himself used to say that this was the most beautiful work ever to come from his hand. The very perceptive talent of his son, Monsignor Pier Filippo Bernini, admiring this most worthy creation wrote the following lines in its praise:

So fair a swoon
Should be immortal;
But since pain does not ascend
To the Divine Presence,
In this stone Bernini made it eternal.

The sinister impressions made by Bernini's rivals on the mind of the Pope were so effective that when Innocent X decided to raise the great obelisk brought to Rome by the Emperor Antoninus Caracalla, which had long been buried at Capo di Bove, and erect it in Piazza Navona as the crowning element of a most noble fountain, he had the leading Roman architects prepare various designs without asking for one from Bernini. But how great a petitioner for its possessor is true merit, and how well it speaks for itself! Prince Niccolò Ludovisi, who was married to a niece of the Pope and who was not only an intimate friend of Bernini but also had influence with him, prevailed on him to make a model of the fountain. In that model Bernini represented the four principal rivers of the world: the Nile for Africa, the Danube for Europe, the Ganges for Asia, and the Río de la Plata for America. A boulder or rock, open in the center, supported the enormous obelisk. Bernini made the model, and the Prince arranged for it to be transported to Palazzo Pamphili in Piazza Navona. There it was secretly placed in a room through which the Pope, who on a certain day was to dine there, had to pass as he left the table. On that very day, which was the Feast of the Annunciation of the Virgin Mary, after the procession the Pope appeared and after the repast went with the Cardinal and Donna Olimpia, his sister-in-law, into that room. Upon seeing such a noble creation and a design for such a vast monument he was nearly ecstatic. Since he was a prince of the clearest intelligence and of the loftiest thoughts, after spending a half an hour or more around the model, continuously admiring and praising it, he burst out in the presence of the whole Secret Council with the following words: "This is a trick of Prince Ludovisi, but it will be necessary to make use of Bernini despite those who do not wish it, since those who do not want his works need not look at them." He immediately sent for Bernini, and with a thousand signs of esteem and love and with a majestic manner, almost apologizing, he explained to him the motives and various reasons for not having made use of him before, and he gave him the commission to make the fountain after his model. Afterward and for the rest of his pontificate, Bernini was always in favor and held in the high esteem to which he was accustomed. Indeed, he was so much in the good graces of that pontiff that every week or so the Pope wanted him at the palace, and there he passed several hours in delightful discourse. It was often said that Bernini was a man born to associate with great princes.

But I do not want to pass too rapidly to other matters without first saying something about the fountain which is counted among Bernini's most marvelous creations and which proved to be one of the most beautiful ornaments of the city of Rome. In the very center, then, of the length and breadth of the great Piazza Navona is situated at ground level a step or bank, so to speak, which forms a great circle about one hundred and six Roman palmi in diameter. About ten palmi from the two extremities lies a great basin symbolizing, I believe, the sea, in the midst of which there rises up to a height of about thirty palmi a mass or, let us say, a grotto made of travertine. This mass is tunnelled through so that from all four sides one can see through to the other side of the piazza. By means of these openings the rock is divided into four parts which are joined and united at the top. These four parts represent the four continents of the world. The sections, by broadening and jutting out in various craggy masses, provide places for four very imposing giant figures of white marble representing the four rivers. The Nile symbolizing Africa is the figure covering the upper part of his head with a cloth as an indication of the obscurity which long prevailed regarding the exact point from which it springs from the earth. Beside it is a very beautiful palm tree. The Danube, which represents Europe, is admiring the marvelous obelisk and has a lion nearby. The Ganges, which stands for Asia, holds a large oar indicating the great extent of its waters. A little below it is a horse. Finally, comes the Río de la Plata for America. It is represented by a Moor, and next to it are some coins to show the wealth of minerals abounding in that country. Beneath the figure is a terrible monster commonly known as the Tatu of the Indies. Around all these river allegories water brought there from the Trevi fountain gushes in great quantities. In the basin at the water line appear some large fish in the act of darting into the sea, all of them most beautiful. One fish on the side toward Piazza Orsini is seen swallowing the water that sustains its life, and having taken in too great a quantity, it blows out the excess—a truly brilliant concept.

The rock mass is made in such a manner that it appears to be a single piece. It cannot be broken into separate pieces through any accident as all the pieces are dovetailed and so placed that one makes bond for the other and all the bonds join to hold the whole together. The pedestal stands splendidly at the exact center of the rock's summit, about twenty-three palmi high. Upon it rests the great obelisk about eighty palmi in height. It is crowned with a beautiful metal finial about ten palmi high upon which a gilded cross shines. Above rests a dove with an olive branch in its beak, the emblem of the Pamphili family. One marvels not a little to see the immense mass of the obelisk erected on a rock so hollowed out and divided and observe how—speaking in artistic terms—it seems to stand upon a void. The water falls in abundance; the sweet murmuring sounds and plenitude make it a thing of utility and delight to the commune. In this great work the entire rock mass, the palm tree, the lion, and half of the horse are completely by Bernini. The Nile is the work of Jacopo Antonio Fancelli, the Ganges by Adamo, the Danube by Andrea Lombardo, and the Río de la Plata by Francesco Baratta. However, in the case of this last large figure and that of the Nile, Bernini made many of the strokes with his own hand.

When this great work was almost completed but before it was unveiled, that is to say, before the scaffolding and the cloth-covered framework which kept it hidden from the public's eye had been removed, the Pope wished to see it. Therefore, one morning the Pope arrived and entered the enclosure together with Cardinal Panzirolo, his secretary of state, and about fifty of his closest confidants. He remained there more than an hour and a half enjoying himself greatly. Since the water had not yet been turned on, the Pope asked Bernini when it would be possible to see it fall. Bernini replied that he could not say on such short notice, since some time was required to put everything in order. Nevertheless, he said he would see to it that everything was done as soon as possible. The pontiff then gave him his benediction and turned toward the door to leave. He had not yet gone out of the enclosure when he heard a loud sound of water. Turning back he saw it gush forth on all sides in great abundance. The Cavalier had, at the crucial moment, given a certain signal to the person whose job it was to open the water ducts, and he quickly had it coursing through the pipes to the mouths of the fountain. Bernini knew that the more unexpected it was, the more pleasing it would be to the Pope. Overcome by such originality and gladdened by so beautiful a sight the Pope returned with his whole court. Turning to Bernini he exclaimed, "In giving us this unexpected joy, Bernini, you have added ten years to our life." As a greater sign of his pleasure the Pope sent to the home of his sister-in-law, Donna Olimpia, in Piazza Navona for a hundred doubloons to be quickly distributed to the men engaged in work on the fountain.

It is impossible to relate how, after the fountain was unveiled, the ideas of the great persons who gathered in that place changed from those they had held before about Bernini, and how he was applauded in public and in private. From that point he became the unique object of the praise of all the academies in Rome. How true it is, as I said before, that those who possess real virtue have nothing to fear.

That work completed, the Pope commissioned Bernini to make the colossal equestrian statue of Constantine for St. Peter's; the pavement of variegated stone for the new part of the church called the Addition of Paul V; and in the same section the bas-reliefs of putti and medallions set into the lateral pilasters and the columns made of cottanella, stone given that name because it was found in a quarry in the Castello di Cottanello in Sabina. The statue was, however, only roughed out at the time of the death of the pontiff. The Pope also wished Bernini to make the model for the altar of the church of S. Francesca Romana and to supervise the restoration of the fountain in front of Palazzo Pamphili in Piazza Navona. For this fountain Bernini carved the statue of Triton with a dolphin entirely by his own hand.

During this period the Most Serene Duke of Modena, Francesco d'Este, wished to have his portrait executed by the hand of Bernini, who carried it out to perfection and sent it to the Duke. He received in silver an honorarium of three thousand scudi for the portrait, while Cosimo Scarlatti, an intimate friend of Bernini who delivered it, was given two hundred gold coins. At about this same time Bernini made his large and very beautiful statue of *Truth Unveiled by Time,* which today one admires in the house of his heirs. It was Bernini's intention to carve also the figure of Time who unveils Truth. He had a large and beautiful piece of marble for this purpose. However, because of his other work he was unable to carry out this resolution and the marble remained as it was when it came from the quarry. He, who in the past months has recorded these things, saw this piece of marble and suddenly, almost as if he wished to sympathize with its misfortune, wrote the following lines and in fun left them with Monsignor Pier Filippo Bernini. We imagine that the marble speaks:

From my ancient rock,
To give me life and voice,
And not only voice and life but also motion, flight,
An artist, unique in this world,
One day drew me forth; his hand once wished
With its busy chisel
And its careful hammer
To strike upon me blows of life
And thus to make of Time a thing stupendous.

But when content and satisfied
To hold the concept in his mind,
He turned aside and said thus to himself:
Will then your hands trained to immortalize
Heroes only be able
To reveal here among us
Glories made ready for a cruel tyrant
Who, in destroying, brings about
So many injuries to art and Nature?
Your most lovely works
Fear perhaps the rigor
Of his hungry tooth.
But to sue for peace
Have you then the need to do him such an honor?
No: because true virtue
Despite the age stays ever whole.
Therefore his hand and gaze
Turned to another object,
And he left off, thinking no more of me.
With him my hope took flight
Of having life, alas, then I lament
That I forever must remain a stone.

As the end of Innocent's pontificate drew near, the old friendship that Bernini had with Monsignor Fabio Chigi became strengthened. It came about in this manner. Monsignor Chigi had just returned from his post as papal nuncio at Cologne. When that prelate went to the Vatican Palace for the first time after his return to Rome, he saw Bernini in the antechamber of Cardinal Pamphili. Recognizing him at once, he greeted him cordially and took him to the rooms that had been assigned to him in that palace. There he kept him for some time, telling him of the great esteem in which his merit was held in Cologne. Bernini was glad to hear himself praised but much gladder to have Monsignor Chigi back and to gain in greater measure the friendship and familiarity of a prelate so worthy and of such high expectations. From that day of mutually exchanged courtesy their friendship grew. When the prelate arrived at the stage where he could don the sacred purple, Bernini undertook the restoration of the Chigi Chapel in S. Maria del Popolo. After the Cardinal became Pope, Bernini executed with his own hand the beautiful marble group of Habakkuk with the Angel and of Daniel in the Lions' Den. At this time Bernini also began work on his plan of the great five-facaded palace for Prince Ludovisi in Piazza Colonna which remained incomplete because of the Pope's death. At the request of the King of Spain, Philip IV, he also made a great bronze crucifix which was placed in the sepulchral Chapel of the Kings.

The sun had not yet set on the day that was Cardinal Chigi's first in the office of Supreme Pontiff when he sent for Cavalier Bernini. With expressions of the utmost affection he encouraged Bernini to embark upon great things in order to carry out the vast plans that he had conceived for the greater embellishment of God's temple, the glorification of the papacy, and the decoration of Rome. Thus he gave Bernini a new and greater trust that never ended during all of his pontificate. Consequently the Pope wished to have Bernini with him every day, to have him mingle with the learned men with whom he adorned his table. The Pope used to say that he was astounded at how Bernini, by the sole force of his genius, could arrive at the point in the discussions that the others had scarcely attained with long study. The Pope named Bernini his own architect, something which the other popes had not done as they all had family architects on whom they wished to confer that post. After Alexander VII this was no longer the case. Because of the respect his successors had of Bernini's singular virtue, he held that post as long as he lived.

I shall now say something of the sumptuous works that this sublime artist executed during the pontificate of Alexander VII, confining myself to a simple account. As I said earlier, the magnificence and originality of these works can only be poorly described. When one actually sees them, they appear quite different from the concept that comes to mind when one has only heard them discussed at length. I mean to say that they can be described only by those who have little observed them. But for those who observe and enjoy them in Rome such a description never hits the mark and rather than being a help may be an impediment.

Bernini was, then, retained by the Pope with a monthly provision of two hundred and sixty scudi. He initiated and in due time finished the colonnade of St. Peter's. In designing this great structure he wished to use an oval plan, thus departing from Michelangelo's design. He did so in order to bring the colonnade closer to the Apostolic Palace and so obstruct less the view of the square from the part of the palace built by Sixtus V with its wing connecting with the Scala Regia. The Scala Regia is also a marvelous work by Bernini and the most difficult he ever executed, for he had to shore up the walls of the Sala Regia and the Pauline Chapel and set both rooms over the vault of the Scala Regia. In the Scala Regia the beautiful perspectives of steps, columns, architraves, pediments, and vaults bring into delightful harmony the stairway's wide entrance and its narrow exit. Bernini used to say that this stairway was the least defective thing he had ever done, and those who saw it before he started work would agree. He felt that the boldest venture he had ever undertaken was to provide support for those walls. He used to say that if, before he began the work, he had read that such a thing had been done by someone else, he would not have believed it.

It was marvelous to see how at the same time Bernini pushed forward the great work of building the colonnade of St. Peter's, he also applied himself on the order of Pope Alexander VII to the creation of the cathedra of St. Peter's which fills the apse of the great Basilica with its richly ornamented mass in fulfillment of the prophecy of Annibale Carracci that we mentioned earlier. He wished that the throne appear to be held aloft by the four great bronze colossi representing the four Doctors of the Church: the two Greek, Gregory of Nazianzus and Athanasius; and the two Latin, Augustine and Ambrose. With inexpressible grace they support the base upon which the cathedra lightly rests. Here, one must admire Bernini's unrivaled patience. After he had made the clay models with great labor by his hands alone, he found that the figures of the Church Fathers were too small. At this point he did not hesitate to do them over in appropriate scale as we see them now. At the order of the same Pope Bernini built the church and dome at Castel Gandolfo; the church at Ariccia, fief of the most excellent House of Chigi; and the Church of S. Andrea at Monte Cavallo in Rome, the Jesuit novitiate. He restored the Church of S. Maria del Popolo and the nearby city gate and erected the annex to the Quirinal Palace for the Pope's family. Making use of an excellent idea, he adapted the Ducal Hall in the Vatican so that it would communicate with the Sala Regia. He built the palace of the Most Eminent Cardinal Chigi, the arsenal in Civitavecchia, and the gallery and the facade facing the sea of the palace at Castel Gandolfo. Besides the statues of Habakkuk and Daniel for the Chigi Chapel which we have already mentioned, at the request of Alexander VII he carved a St. Jerome and a St. Mary Magdalen. He made the model of the Pope's statue which was placed in the Siena Cathedral. In this work he was assisted by his disciple Antonio Raggi, called the Lombard, who made the finished sculpture. Now that the colossal marble statue of Constantine on horseback was carried to completion, it was placed at the foot of the stairway of St. Peter's.

It was in the beginning of this pontificate that there appeared in Rome, veiled in a new and beautiful light, the royal majesty of Christina, the great Queen of Sweden. She was always then and is now a true tutelary spirit of the artists in that palace of the world. There was thus opened to Cavalier Bernini a wide path to the enjoyment of the benign influence of that star. Bernini was present with others of the Pope's family at the most solemn ceremony in which he and all Rome gathered to meet the monarch. Bernini had already engaged the royal mind through his widespread fame. The Queen had gained such a strong impression of him that from the time of their first conversations she began to demonstrate those qualities and aspects that a great person who is also outstanding in every virtue knows how to employ with those who are truly brilliant. We will have more to say about this during the course of this history.

In the year 1664 by the Roman calendar, before the end of March, the King of France, Louis XIV, decided to restore his palace, the Louvre, and to enlarge it with regal magnificence. His own architects had already provided him with ideas, but the King, wishing the design to be carried out in conformity with his own lofty taste which could only be satisfied with that which would be admired by all eyes, even the most erudite, wanted to have the opinion of our artist. He therefore had M. Colbert, one of his principal ministers, write as follows:

Monsieur,

The rare products of your spirit which make you admired by the whole world and of which the King, my master, has a complete knowledge will not permit him to finish his superb and magnificent edifice of the Louvre without showing the plans to one as excellent as yourself in order to obtain your opinion. It is for this reason that he has commanded me to write you these lines, in order to urge you on his behalf to give some part of those hours which you spend with such glory in the embellishment of the world's first city, to look at the plans which will be presented to you by Monsignor, the Abbot Elpidio Benedetti. His Majesty hopes that you will not only make your opinions known to him, but also that you will put on paper some of those admirable ideas which to you are so habitual and of which you have given so much evidence. He wishes that you have complete faith in all that the previously mentioned abbot will tell you on his part regarding this subject. Moreover, I hope you will be pleased with what I am submitting by word of mouth through him. I assure you in these few lines that I am truly,

Monsieur,

Your Most Humble and Most Respectful Servant
Colbert

On the receipt of such a commission and after he had studied the plans and drawings that were sent to him, Bernini went to work on the design. When he had finished it, he sent it to the King. Meanwhile, he continued the work on the cathedra and the colonnade of St. Peter's. I shall not accept as proof of how much Bernini's designs for the palace pleased the King the very valuable gift he sent: his portrait strewn with diamonds valued at three thousand scudi. Any attempt to use this gift to evaluate the King's esteem would be subject to error, since the value of the gift could be attributed solely to the royal and unique generosity of that great monarch. I would rather cite the letter that the King sent to the artist in testimony of his esteem and even more the letter he wrote to the Pope. I will, as usual, quote both of them here, adding another letter to the Most Eminent Cardinal Chigi and also one that M. Colbert had written to Bernini earlier.

The letter of His Majesty the King:

Signor Cavalier Bernini,

I have such a special esteem for your merit that I have a great desire to see and to know more closely a personage so illustrious if my intention is compatible with your service to the

Holy Father and with your own convenience. My desire moves me to dispatch this special courier to Rome to ask you to give me the gratification of undertaking the journey to France on the propitious occasion of the return of my cousin, the Duke of Créqui, who is my special ambassador. He will explain to you in greater detail the urgent reason that causes me to wish to see and discuss with you the fine designs that you have sent me for the building of the Louvre. For the rest, as I have told my cousin, I will make my good intentions known to you. I pray God that he keep you, Signor Cavalier Bernini, in His holy care.

From Lyons.
Written in Paris, 11 April 1665.

Louis

Letter from the Most Christian King to the Pope:

Most Holy Father, having already received by order of Your Holiness two designs for my building of the Louvre from a hand so distinguished as that of the Cavalier Bernini, I should think rather of thanking you for this favor instead of requesting still another favor of you. But since it regards a building that for many centuries has been the principal residence of the kings who are the most zealous in all Christendom in the support of the Holy See, I believe that I may apply to Your Holiness in all confidence. I entreat you then, if his duty to you permits it, to command the Cavalier to come here in order to finish his work. Your Holiness could not grant me a greater favor in the present set of circumstances. I will add that it could not be made to anyone who feels more veneration or more warmth than I,
Most Holy Father.

Paris, 18 April 1665.

Your Most Devoted Son
Louis

From the King of France to the Most Eminent Cardinal Chigi:

My Cousin,

I have taken the liberty of writing to His Holiness to thank him for the designs that Cavalier Bernini made for the construction of the Louvre and also to entreat him to command Bernini to come here in order to finish his work. How I hope that His Holiness will be pleased to give this order. I have sent letters ahead so that upon entering my kingdom Bernini will begin to receive some proof through the manner in which he is treated of the consideration I have for his merit. In regard to the designs, you have obliged me with so much kindness that I can look forward to no other outcome from the continuation of your good offices with His Holiness than the fulfillment of my prayers. I urgently implore it of you, and again I confirm that I hold always for your person all the affection and esteem that you could desire. I pray that God will assist you,

My Cousin.

Paris, 10 April 1665.

Louis

Letter from M. Colbert to Cavalier Bernini:

My Lord,

I decided not to write about the superb design for the Louvre that you sent to me until the King had carefully studied it and given his opinion. But since he let it be known only a little while ago that the beauty of your concept corresponds perfectly with your great and universal reputation, I believe I would do wrong to the judgment of such a great Prince and to yourself as well if I did not give you a report of it. This has prompted me to write you this letter. I also want to tell you that, having shown the design to Signor Cardinal Chigi at his legation and by royal order making a like observation, His Eminence has on his return to Rome assumed the responsibility of speaking to you concerning it and of encouraging you to new efforts in this great work. If it is agreeable to you, I will refer this matter to the conference that His Eminence will have with you. Meanwhile, I remain, with most sincere respect,

Vincennes, 3 October 1664,

Your Most Humble and Most Affectionate Servant
Colbert

The King's letters arrived after the Duke of Créqui, Royal Ambassador in Rome, had already taken official leave of His Holiness. He had been about to depart when it became necessary for him to put in another appearance. With his customary pomp he went to the Vatican Palace to present the letters to the Pope. He then went to Bernini's house to give him his letters and to explain the wish of his master that he undertake the journey to France, not only for the building of the Louvre, but also because His Majesty wished to have a portrait of himself by Bernini, that is, a head and bust. Bernini was both happy and fearful at so great a summons. Joy urged him to go and pluck the fruits of his long and unceasing labors by accepting the great honor that monarch offered him in calling him to his service. But fear constricted his heart at the thought of the imminent dangers of such a long voyage as he was then about sixty-eight years old. He found himself, therefore, in great anxiety which his dearest friend, Father Gian Paolo Oliva, knew how to handle with care, eloquence, and love. Father Oliva was the General of the Society of Jesus, that noble order, one of the glories of our century. Father Oliva, following his own instincts, wishing to please the King and impelled by the importunities of Cardinal Antonio Barberini who was acting in the King's name, entered into the negotiations. After leavening Bernini's justifiable fears with hope, he asserted that to submit to such a summons, even at the cost of life itself, was an admirable action. Bernini then, without further thought, made up his mind and resolved to leave. His Holiness the Pope gave his consent to please the King, above all in conformance with the proprieties then practiced with that monarch. He sent the following brief in reply to the King's letter:

The Brief of the Pope to the Most Christian King:

Pope Alexander VII to our Louis, Most Christian King of the French, most beloved in Christ the Son.

Cherished son, the noble Duke Créqui, your Majesty's spokesman, has delivered your message to us and has very earnestly requested that we should grant the presence in your kingdom of our dear son Cavalier Bernini for three months. Although this request would scarcely be granted because his assistance is now necessary for the construction of the Vatican colonnades and for other requirements of St. Peter's building program, nevertheless, because the magnitude of our love for you overcomes all, we have granted it with a glad heart. So we bestow on Your Majesty the Apostolic Benediction especially brought forth from all the sentiment of the paternal heart.

Given at Rome in S. Maria Maggiore with the seal of the Fisherman's Ring, April 23, 1665, in the eleventh year of our pontificate.

Bernini left Rome April 25, 1665, to the sorrow and anxiety of the whole city. It was thought that because of the dangers of the journey he would be lost to Rome. The fear also spread among the people that the King by his royal munificence might be able to keep Bernini with him by offering him conditions that he could scarcely allow himself to refuse. Paolo, Bernini's second son, accompanied him on the trip as did Mattia de' Rossi, Bernini's favorite assistant, a very courteous, well-mannered young man, who was well known for his architectural talent, and Giulio Cesare, another of Bernini's pupils in sculpture. The head of the King's household, the forerunner of the King, and other servants accompanied Bernini at the monarch's expense. Throughout the journey Bernini received honors that surpass description from all the princes. Most notable of all was the reception of Ferdinand, the Grand Duke of Tuscany, of glorious memory. During the few days that Bernini stayed in Florence the Duke commended him to the care of Gabbriello Riccardi, Marquis of Chianni and Rivalto, a cavalier of great merit and extraordinary wealth. Riccardi had served with nobility and splendor for eighteen years, first as ambassador to His Most Catholic Majesty, the King of Spain, and then to His Holiness the Pope. He then served as councilor of state and majordomo. The Marquis received Bernini in grand fashion in his noble palace at the corner of Via Larga, formerly the residence of their Serene Highnesses, the Grand Dukes of Tuscany. Among the glorious ancestors of the house who lived there were Alessandro de' Medici, the First Duke, and Cosimo de' Medici, the First Grand Duke of Tuscany. In this palace and the palace of the Marquis' garden in the street called Gualfonda, Bernini was able to see as much beauty as his genius could desire. Besides pictures of great value there were in the palace seventy-one busts and eight complete statues. In the garden there were two hundred and ten busts and six complete statues, all precious remains of ancient Greece and Rome, as well as the marvelous bronze head and neck of a horse that by common consensus and also in the opinion of Bernini, is by the same hand as the famous horse of the Capitoline. There were also statues by the finest masters of modern times. Bernini remained a few days in Florence in order to see the most beautiful things of his native land. Finally he took leave of the Grand Duke who wished that he be accompanied by his own litter as far as the Italian frontier. His Most Serene Highness the Duke of Savoy unceasingly gave the Cavalier proof of his generosity also. His actions in this were in keeping with the grandeur of his spirit. In every place that Bernini had to pass through the word of his presence spread, so that cities were depopulated by the townspeople's desire to come out and see him. He said in jest that it was as if he were a traveling elephant.

On word of his arrival at Pont-de-Beauvoisin in France the local officials came out to meet him as the King had ordered, and one of them delivered a welcoming address. He received similar honors in all the other cities and places of that most fortunate kingdom from then on. Bernini responded in an easy affable way. The gifts he received he had distributed to various charities. When he was still over three miles from Lyons he was met by all the painters, sculptors, and engineers of the city, some on horseback and some in carriages. Three days before his arrival in Paris he found the King's litter awaiting him on landing. He was still over three miles from the city when Monsignor Roberti, the apostolic nuncio, came to meet him in his own carriage drawn by the King's horses. He took Bernini to the Louvre where noble lodgings had been prepared for him. On his arrival the Cavalier found it necessary to seek immediately the repose of a bed after the discomforts of the trip in the carriage. But just when he had somewhat rested himself, M. Colbert appeared to visit him on behalf of the King, who was impatiently awaiting him at St. Germain. Bernini remained in Paris the following day seeing all he could of the Louvre and the great city of Paris and then departed for St. Germain. The applause and congratulations that persons of stature offered to our artist in the King's antechamber were equal to the affection, the esteem, and the warmth that he had received in Paris. He was talked about so much everywhere that it was said that during this period there was no mode in Paris but Bernini. No longer being able to stand the delay, the great monarch appeared at the door. The presentation was made in the midst of all those great men. The King conversed with

Bernini more than half an hour. For the most part the monarch spoke of the great regard he had for Bernini's talent and his desire to make public acknowledgment of it. When Bernini took leave of the King, it was time for dinner, and he and his son were given a place at the table of the princes and chief ministers of the kingdom.

Bernini stayed in Paris for six months during which time he made the plans for the Louvre and laid the foundations for the building. He then put his hand to the portrait of the King. It must be stated that there were so many ladies, princes, and cavaliers visiting him during this period that it was necessary for him to leave his lodgings in the Louvre and go to the palace of Cardinal Mazarin where the distractions were less. The King favored Bernini with demonstrations of familiarity and was often happy to serve as a living model. Once when the King had been standing for an hour, Bernini threw down his chisel in admiration and loudly exclaimed, "Miracle, miracle that a King so meritorious, youthful, and French should remain immobile for an hour."

One day when that monarch was arranging himself in his customary way to pose for a drawing, Bernini came up to him and gently parted the locks of hair which were arranged, as was the fashion, over the brow. He exposed the forehead somewhat and in an almost authoritative manner said: "Your Majesty is a king who must show his forehead to one and all." It was charming to see how in a flash all the court followed that hair style, which from then on was called "the Bernini modification."

The base Bernini made for his noble likeness of the king provided the opportunity for a fine mind to compose the following lines:

Bernini wracked his brains for the right thing
To hold the bust of this so great king,
And then at last, having found none at all,
Spoke thus: For such a King the world's too small.

As the glory of our artist grew in the city of Paris and in all France where his name was everywhere, so his fame spread also throughout Italy and especially Rome, where Father Oliva received from M. de Lionne letters relating quite specifically how very much His Majesty enjoyed this great man. To remove every suspicion of hyperbole and exaggeration, I will make it obvious through the letters that Father Oliva wrote in reply to M. de Lionne along with his letter of the same period to Bernini. They are as follows:

To the Marquis de Lionne, Paris.

With too great an amplitude of honors and of sentiment the Most Christian King acknowledges that small homage rendered by me to the grandeur of his monarchy and to the sublimity of his talent. It is true that I pleaded with the Cavalier Bernini to go into the service of such a King, even if it were certain that he should lose his life in the Alps. But such a suggestion, so manifestly correct, merited neither the affectionate approval of His Majesty nor the warm expressions of Your Excellency, since it sufficed to be a man and not a truncated statue to note the incomparable honor that redounded to the name of the architect by so glorious a summons. In such considerations, which are so true in themselves and so well known to me, lie the measure of the excess of my indebtedness to the King. This indebtedness obliges me to live for him for as long as I live. Inexpressibly, then, do I rejoice that the presence of the Cavalier near his Majesty has not lessened his hope nor reduced his fame. To such a man I am under obligation, bound by a most tender affection that directs me and by the goodwill which obtains for me such great influence with him, so that when he told me of the summons to go to France while at the same time retreating from it because of all the dangers of the voyage, I alone urged him with such force to go that all the ice of Mont Cenis melted from the atmosphere of the royal invitation in his mind. I cannot but rejoice to see him over there with the esteem that he has always enjoyed here. Although in the glorious splendor of his art he is the prince among all, yet I believe that he possesses many other aspects of understanding and wisdom in his soul which might almost eclipse that excellence for which the world admires him. Therefore, I confess I am no less indebted to your kindness for the assurances you have given me of the King's approval of what I have done, than for the news you have given me of that gentleman in the advancement of his reputation. I will wait to unfold to you in another letter the great esteem in which I hold Your Excellency, both for your letter of the 8th and for that which the Cavalier writes here.

Marquis de Lionne, Paris

Cavalier Bernini writes to his son, the Monsignor, of being struck by the esteem in which Your Excellency holds me as well as by the love it pleases you to bestow upon me. I lacked the courage in my previous letter to join to that discussion, so full of references to royal favors, the outpouring of thanks to one so venerated by me. But I say to you that the honor you have done me is of such high value that your pen, even in confrontation with the royal benignity, expressed it to me with such energy of style that it retains its value and obtains from my heart such an inalterable gratitude that I have no formula to express it. Know, then, that in the pleasing of a King I have not considered his crown but his person. To me His Highness glitters so in distinctions and loving concept that I am forgetful of the King's sublime ministers to whom others, spellbound, bow, in order to be carried away by the ecstasy of the contemplation of the marvels of his personal qualities. The supreme fortune that you enjoy in the confidence of so highly acclaimed a monarch becomes minimal when compared to his great merit. Nor do I say this in order to put on paper a pleasing sentence. I write thus because I see it to be the common sentiment of those who have knowledge of European affairs. Though I am indeed blind or see very little in these matters, nevertheless, I know clearly how to yield to the immense ability, the breadth and depth of administrative wisdom of Your Excellency. Though I know very well how to name the office of the person to whom my other epistolary efforts are directed, with yours I omit the title of Prime Minister and First Secretary of the Most Christian King: the name Marquis de Lionne is sufficient. By the gifts of your great spirit you have risen above the envied fortune of your high offices which, among those of good judgment, are to be preferred over many others, even crowned commanders, since they serve a sovereign of such renown.

Cavalier Bernini, Paris.

I have already confessed my great obligation to your hand which has crowned my book with that miracle of a drawing. But now I owe almost more to your tongue which has gained me the thanks of the King of France, so famous and so celebrated throughout the earth. It was too great a sign of love for you to have reached the royal ear with what I told you in the very serious and private talk in which we both determined that you should go to Paris even if the journey should cost you your life. It never crossed my mind that the energy with which I detached you from the arms of your sons and dried the tears of your family would become known to anyone. My reward was in having served you and in having urged you into that arena of honor and to that immortality of name that you could not enjoy if you had not personally enrolled yourself in the service of so venerated a ruler. I spoke in order to serve you. You were pleased to think of me too highly, bringing me—a respectful admirer—to the attention of a prince who overthrew Calvinism, who abolished duelling, who richly rewarded merit, who undertook to join the Ocean to the Mediterranean, an enterprise not even undertaken by the ancient Romans, lords of the earth. Among his antecedents he is last in number as he is, undoubtedly, first in acclaim. From this I can see his perspicacity, which I serve with all my heart, and the good fortunes I desire for you. These will be superior to my strongest wishes, since they come from a King who in magnificence surpasses the imagination of those he loves and the merits of those who serve him, as you do in preparing for him a royal residence whose foundations will bury the ancient memories of the palaces of the Caesars. Your son, the most illustrious Monsignor, continues to live here in the same good and intelligent manner as when you left. That will allow you to live quietly and contentedly even though far from Rome.

Meanwhile there was much talk in Rome. The great men of the court, as well as people of minor account, and even the Pope expected to hear at any moment the news that Bernini would stay in Paris. To be truthful, Bernini was no less concerned himself. Gratitude toward the Holy See and the person of the Pope impelled his heart to decline the requests to remain there. He felt that the various offers made to him worked against him and his whole house. Not the least of these considerations was the opportunity to arrange his son's marriage to a noblewoman with a rich dowry. Nevertheless, the Pope did not impose a time limit nor use the occasion to urge him to return. That was done by the Most Eminent

Cardinal Chigi, who offered reasons of necessity and affection. These reasons are clear in the phrases of a letter that he wrote to Bernini August 4, 1665.

Most Illustrious Signore,

I congratulate Your Lordship infinitely for having made such a beautiful plan of the Louvre and for having so pleased His Majesty, whose perfect taste makes his approval the more impressive. I hear that you are going to make the King's portrait; I am sorry that you will not have the proper marble even though Your Lordship's genius will shine forth equally in any marble. I hope that in working on this portrait you will not go beyond the time conceded to you by Our Lord, since your absence brings suffering here not only to the buildings but to all of us who are deprived of your conversation. Thanks to the trouble that your brother Luigi took with it, the facade of my house is coming along well. I can give you a fine report of your son, the Monsignor, whose judgment conforms to the generosity of his spirit.

At the end of the letter he added in his own hand:

Continue, Your Lordship, to give me news of your health. I thank you for it and congratulate you on it. But I am much more delighted in the applause all France gives you, applause which increases our envy and our desire to see you back here. The hour is now drawing close when you shall return and again see beautiful Italy and those who impatiently await you.

Giovan Lorenzo finally satisfied the wishes of His Majesty in all respects regarding the plan for the palace and the portrait.

The King was pleased to concede to his departure for the return to Italy. He accompanied his permission with an honorarium appropriate to his royal magnificence. Bernini received twenty thousand scudi and an annual pension for life of another two thousand. A similar pension of five hundred scudi was assigned to Paolo, his son. Mattia de' Rossi, his assistant, received twenty-five hundred scudi in a lump sum with the stipulation that he promise to return to France whenever necessary to put in effect the Cavalier's design. This he was later on obliged to do. Giulio Cesare, Bernini's young sculptor, received one thousand scudi. There was not a person, unimportant as he might be, down to the stable boys, who was not royally compensated before departing in accordance with his rôle. In the mind of a magnanimous prince, each man is worthy in relation to what he can do: a lofty conception and regard for value.

Bernini then left Paris with Paolo his son, who carved and left in France a marble figure of Christ as a boy in the act of piercing his hand with a thorn. Bernini's assistants, Mattia de' Rossi and Giulio Cesare, as well as the usual entourage supplied by and at the expense of the King, followed him to Rome.

There were great festivities at the court at Bernini's return and all Italy rejoiced, for she felt herself to be part of his glory for having produced such a man, one who was called into the service of so great a King. When General Oliva, who played so large a rôle in ironing out for Bernini the difficulties of the voyage, heard, during the cordial conversations he had with him, of the favors Bernini had received from the King, he could not restrain himself from showing his own satisfaction by writing the following lines to the Marquis de Lionne:

Cavalier Bernini has arrived in Rome transformed into the trumpet of the Most Christian King, who has almost turned the sculptor to stone, so struck is he by His Majesty's incomparable gifts. His overwhelming wonder, both in his gratitude for the unheard of honors and enormous help given him, as well as for his admiration of the greatness and the magnanimity of such a king, has made him feel totally incapable of expressing his gratitude. For in order to celebrate a monarch of such high merit he must go beyond the King's birth and dominion, declaring that he is far more sublime because of his mental capacity, his prudent speech, the splendor of his power, the generosity of his heart, the justice demanded in his tribunals, and his majesty in every respect—which is not great, considering the vastness of his dominion and the power of his arms—which make him the equal of the most celebrated kings in the annals of antiquity. Truly, I do not know if a man so favored could with more tender affection and more reverence of feeling so love and magnify his benefactor with perpetual and heartfelt expresison than does that gentleman who has been immortalized by His Majesty in the memory of posterity and in the pages of chroniclers. From him I received confirmation of your manifestation of love and esteem for me. I do not merit this because of the weakness of my qualities, which are too dissimilar to your own. Yet I claim the affection that it brings which (if you permit such great temerity) I equal or better. I am only sorry that the fruitfulness of my affection and feelings for your merit is equalled by the dearth of works for your benefit. Such dearth is not due to any lack of desire to perform them, but because I am unable to do so—so slight in me are those qualities which in you, among the greatest, are so great.

Prior to his journey to Paris Bernini had been commissioned by the monarch to make a great marble statue of him, life-size and on horseback, to be placed in Paris. Therefore, Bernini started to work on a great single block of stone which was said to be the largest that had ever been struck by a chisel up to then. In the space of four years he executed the great figure of the King on horseback, which today can still be seen in the rooms adjoining the basilica of St. Peter's. The great monarch is represented in an attitude that is both majestic and benign. He almost seems to be riding up a steep cliff. The artist wished to signify by this device that only by the precipitous and rugged road of virtue does one reach the place of true glory. And it cannot be left unsaid that the King, in order to give new signs of satisfaction and of esteem to our artist, had a beautiful medal cast with his portrait on one side. On the reverse there were allegories of painting, sculpture, architecture, and mathematics in charming attitudes with their proper attributes and emblems and the motto: SINGULARIS IN SINGULIS, IN OMNIBUS UNICUS.

Together with the royal munificence of Louis in France went equally the acts of generosity of Alexander in Rome, who along with the compensation given to Bernini honored the person of Pier Filippo, his eldest son who belonged to the priesthood, with honorable duties and a canonry of S. Maria Maggiore, along with various ecclesiastical prebends. Two times the Pope went in person to Bernini's house. Such was the esteem in which he held Bernini that he was in the habit of saying that nature, in order to make him altogether unique, had given him great genius and extraordinary wisdom and that painting, sculpture, and architecture were the lesser part of his excellence and in this regard it was sufficient to say that he lived during the pontificate of Alexander VII.

That pontiff was succeeded by Giulio Rospigliosi, who took the name of Clement IX. Bernini had been quite a good friend of the pontiff since the days of Urban VIII, for Giulio Rospigliosi, among his other gifts, had a special talent for beautiful and noble poetry. Thus it fell to him to compose the dramas which the prince-nephews of Urban VIII staged for the wholesome entertainment and the happiness of the Roman people. These performances were presented with music, with scenery on which were painted beautiful views, with the most ingenious stage machinery showing great imagination, and with all Cavalier Bernini's assistance. Therefore, from that period on Giulio Rospigliosi could gain a good idea of the artist's genius and worth because of continuous intimate discussions about these matters with him. So he, too, on the very first day of his elevation sent for Bernini and bestowed on him heartfelt expressions of his love.

The Pope was not in good health and was so troubled by insomnia that for some time he had tried to induce sleep by listening to the murmur of water. For this reason he ordered Bernini to remove every impediment to the free flow of the water in the Belvedere fountain (above which the windows of the Pope's chambers opened) so that all the gushing of water could be heard when it was needed for his indisposition. The Cavalier set to work, but in the execution of his plan it happened that not only was he unable to increase the flow of water, but that the little there was, was dispersed in another direction. What could Bernini do in such a situation? Something truly new and ingenious, that much, indeed, can be said. He quickly invented a machine and put it in the room next to the one in which the Pope slept. The machine moved a wheel that upon striking certain paper globes with multiple blows made a sound exactly like a very abundant fountain. Thus he supplanted the missing fountain for that night and satisfied the Pope's need. On hearing of it the day after, as he had not known how things had been arranged, the Pope could not stop saying that Bernini's genius always expressed itself in little things as well as great. And when Bernini was in the Pope's presence he said to him with his characteristic graciousness and loving affability: "Truly, Signor Cavalier Bernini, we would never have believed that on the first day of our pontificate we would be deceived by you."

Clement IX followed the custom of Alexander VII and Urban VIII by engaging Bernini in conversation at the dinner hour, but, however, with the difference that Clement ordinarily wished no other person present. He usually dined late in the morning and he never permitted Bernini to go without letting him know by some warm remark how great a pleasure he derived from this so great an inconvenience to him (Bernini was already in his declining years). One day, distracted by I know not what worry, he was about to let Bernini go without a word. When the Pope observed that Bernini hesitated, he asked him if there was something he wished. Bernini replied: "Forgive me, Holy Father, I am so accustomed to receiving from Your Holiness some word of consolation on leaving that I cannot bring myself to depart without it." This incident was most pleasing to Clement, who recognized through it the great esteem in which Bernini held the honor of being with him. The pontiff also wished to go in person to see Bernini's works in his house by the Church of S. Andrea delle Fratte, following the example of his predecessors. On one of these occasions the following episode occurred: The Pope, having satisfied his honest curiosity, was preparing to leave when Bernini's wife and his daughters, two of whom were nuns of S. Ruffina (a convent that did not belong to a closed order), wished to take advantage of the occasion to kiss the Pope's feet. The pontiff seemed to become rather disturbed at this action, nor for the time being could they discover why. However, they soon understood, for that very evening a servant of His Holiness appeared at Bernini's house with a purse filled with gold medals and orders to distribute them to Bernini's daughters and to his household. Therefore, Bernini held that the reason for the Pope's discomfiture could be nothing else than finding himself in a situation where he was unable to demonstrate to Bernini and his family his paternal love and royal generosity.

During the pontificate of Clement IX, Bernini finished the right wing of the portico of St. Peter's by the Holy Office and the ramp or, as we would say, the pavilion in front of the basilica of St. Peter's. He embellished the bridge of Sant'Angelo with statues of angels carrying instruments of Christ's passion and designed the balustrades. Bernini made with his own hand two of the angels that were to be placed with the others on the bridge. But it did not seem right to Pope Clement that such beautiful works should remain there exposed to damage from the weather. Therefore, he had copies of them made. The originals were placed elsewhere at the disposition of the cardinal-nephew. Nevertheless, Bernini carved another angel secretly, the one with the superscription, so that a work for the Pope, to whom he knew he owed so much, would not be without some work by his hand. When the Pope learned of it, although he was very pleased, he said, "In short, Cavalier, you wish to compel me to have yet another copy made." And let my reader now consider that Bernini though well on in years carved three entire marble statues, larger than life-size, in the space of two years: a thing that to those most competent in art seemed to be an impossibility.

Rome and the entire world mourned the death of Clement IX. Cardinal Emilio Altieri succeeded him as Clement X. Because of his great age (he was then eighty-one years old) the new Pope was unable to entertain the idea of building or of adorning the city. This gave Bernini the opportunity to rest his mind and body, worn out from the incessant labors that, for the general benefit, he had sustained for seventy years and more. That, however, did not stop the Pope's nephew, Cardinal Altieri, from availing himself as much as possible of Bernini's work. He commissioned him to make a portrait of His Holiness and the beautiful statue of the Blessed Lodovica Albertoni in the throes of death, which is admired today in the sumptuous chapel in S. Francesco a Ripa. During that reign Bernini also made the multicolored marble floor of the arcade of St. Peter's and in the basilica itself the ciborium of bronze and lapis lazuli for the Chapel of the Sacrament with its two bronze angels in the act of adoring the Host which is kept therein. In the same place one can see the beautiful panel with scenes from the life of St. Maurice. It was painted by Bernini, and not by his assistant, Carlo Pellegrino, as everyone says. This panel, placed in front of the beautiful works of sculpture by the same artist, leaves us in great uncertainty as to whether Bernini made his name shine more brilliantly in painting or in statuary art. For this chapel he also made the designs for the pavement and the balustrade.

During Alexander VII's lifetime Cavalier Bernini had made a design and a model completely by his own hand of the Pope's tomb to be placed in St. Peter's. These had received the approval not only of His Eminence Cardinal Chigi, the Pope's nephew, but of Alexander VII, himself, who ordered Bernini to complete the whole project. When Clement X died and Innocent XI, who most blessedly rules today, was elevated to the papal throne, Bernini applied himself diligently to the tomb and brought it to conclusion. In this tomb Bernini's genius shines forth with its customary vitality. He set the tomb in a great niche containing a door through which there is a continual coming and going. But he made such good use of the door; which to others would have seemed a great impediment, that it served him as an aid, or rather, a necessary component for working out his splendid concept. What Bernini did was to create the illusion that the door was covered by a great pall. This he carved of Sicilian jasper. On the pall in gilded bronze is Death emerging from the door and lifting the pall with which she covers her head, almost as if in shame. At the same time she extends an arm out toward the figure of Pope Alexander VII, who is represented above by a kneeling marble figure twice life-size. Death demonstrates by the hour glass in her hand that, for the Pope, time has run out. At the bottom of the tomb on either side are two large marble figures, one representing Charity, the other Truth. This latter figure was completely nude, though the nudity was concealed somewhat by the play of the pall about her and also by the sun which covered some of the bosom. But a nude woman, even though of stone and by Bernini's hand, was unsuitable to the purity of mind of the present Pope, Innocent XI. He let it be known in a gracious way that it would be to his liking if Bernini would cover her somewhat in whatever manner seemed best to him.

Bernini quickly made her a garment of bronze which he tinted white to look like marble. For him it was a work of immense thought and labor, as he had to unite one thing to another that had been made with a different aim in mind. He held, however, that it was effort well spent, since by these measures, and by that beautiful example, the holiness of mind of that great Pope would shine forth for all the centuries to come. In the upper part of the tomb are two other statues of which we see only the upper half. They are Justice and Prudence. The whole tomb is crowned by the arms of the Pope, placed over the gilded niche and sustained by two great wings.

Bernini was already in the eightieth year of his life. For some time past he had been turning his most intense thoughts to attaining eternal repose rather than to increasing his earthly glory. Also, deep within his heart was the desire to offer, before closing his eyes to this life, some sign of gratitude to Her Majesty the Queen of Sweden, his most special patron. In order, therefore, to penetrate more deeply into the first concept and to prepare himself better for the second, he set to work with the greatest intensity to create a half-length figure, larger than life-size of Our Saviour Jesus Christ.

This is the work that he said was his favorite and it was the last given the world by his hand. He meant it as a gift for the monarch, but in this intention he was unsuccessful. The Queen's opinion of, and esteem for, the statue was so great that, not finding herself in circumstances in which it was possible to give a comparable gift in exchange, she chose to reject it rather than fail in the slightest degree to equal the royal magnificence of Bernini's spirit. Bernini, therefore, as we will relate in the proper place, had to leave it to her in his will. In this divine image he put all the force of his Christian piety and of art itself. In it he proved the truth of his familiar axiom, that the artist with a truly strong foundation in drawing and design need fear no diminution of vitality, sensitivity, or other good qualities in his work when he reaches old age; for thanks to this sureness in design, he is able to make up fully for those defects which tend to petrify under the weight of years. This, he said, he had observed in other artists.

Thus, Giovan Lorenzo, continuing to create beautiful works, remained his old self. But Heaven which had always found the acts of his spirit no less worthy than the deeds of his hand, in order to test once more his constancy, set new storms moving against him in Rome—storms truly capable of making any heart tremble, but not, as experience has earlier shown, his own. It happened, then, that invidious tongues and, perhaps, also the feeble chatter of small people about some imaginary new cracks in St. Peter's dome, spread a whispering campaign throughout Italy. The report foolishly held that these cracks were caused by the niches under the relics, and by other alleged works which they said Bernini had made during the reign of Urban VIII in the piers that carry the dome. These whisperings, which in the beginning were no more than little sparks of slander, soon flared into such a conflagration that a clamor went up not just in Rome but in all of Europe as well. To men of little understanding it seemed that because of those cracks each day could be the one on which the dome would fall. To the less credulous it seemed an act of extraordinary discretion to concede it some few months of life. Bernini who, on the contrary, understood the game well, knew the false foundations of the rumor. He, therefore, did not permit himself to grieve over it. Moreover, he gained in courage and strength of heart. But every day these whisperings spread and became worse. Among the rabble they continued until Bernini's death, and even yet they now and then speak of it. It is our task today to destroy this deception. This I will do further along in the narration. I will give a precise account of the whole history along with the necessary proof, not drawn, certainly, from my own observations of the sites, which I visited several times with men who have complete mastery of such material, but drawn from the noble efforts, studies, and observations of the celebrated Mattia de' Rossi, who is today director of the Fabbrica of St. Peter's and also architect of St. Peter's, an office previously held by Cavalier Bernini.

During the very period when these discussions were going on in Rome the ancient Chancellery Palace actually began to threaten to collapse. The Pope, therefore, ordered Bernini to repair the damage. He applied himself quickly to the task with all his energies. Since every day he found new and great difficulties that required much thought and labor to overcome, he had to exert himself greatly, often climbing up and down the scaffolding, in short subjecting himself to work much too heavy for his advanced age. Try as they would his own sons could not dissuade him from exposing himself to the great danger of overexertion. He said that he investigated as much and no less than the work and his own reputation required, and he wished to do his duty to both even at the cost of his life. And while the city of Rome was preparing to acclaim him on the propitious outcome of the restoration and strengthening of the palace, Bernini had already begun to lose sleep, and his strength and spirits were at such a low ebb that within a brief time he was brought to the end of his days.

But before speaking of his last illness and death, which to our eyes truly seemed like his life, we should here mention that, although it may be that up until his fortieth year, the age at which he married, Cavalier Bernini had some youthful romantic entanglements without, however, creating any impediment to his studies of the arts or prejudicing in any way that which the world calls prudence, we may truthfully say that his marriage not only put an end to this way of living, but that from that hour he began to behave more like a cleric than a layman. So spiritual was his way of life that, according to what was reported to me by those who know, he might often have been worthy of the admiration of the most perfect monastics. He always kept fixed in his mind an intense awareness of death. He often had long discussions on this subject with Father Marchesi, his nephew who was an Oratorian priest at the Chiesa Nuova, known for his goodness and learning.

So great and continual was the fervor with which he longed for the happiness of that last step, that for the sole intention of attaining it, he frequented for forty years continuously the devotions conducted toward this end by the fathers of the Society of Jesus in Rome. There, also, he partook of the Holy Eucharist twice a week.

He increased the alms which he had been accustomed to give from his earliest youth. He became absorbed at times in the thoughts and in the expression of the profound reverence and understanding that he always had of the efficacy of the Blood of Christ the Redeemer, in which, he was wont to say, he hoped to drown his sins. He made a drawing of this subject, which he then had engraved and printed. It shows the image of Christ Crucified, with streams of blood gushing from his hands and feet forming almost a sea, and the great Queen of Heaven who offers it to God the Father. He also painted this pious concept on a great canvas which he wanted always to have facing his bed in life and in death.

His time then came; I do not know whether I should say expected because of his great loss of strength or because of his yearning for the eternal repose that he had so long desired. He was ill of a slow fever followed at the end by an attack of apoplexy which took his life. Throughout it all he was very patient and resigned to the Divine Will. Nor did he as a rule converse about anything but his trust in it. His words were so striking that those in attendance, among whom Cardinal Azzolino did not disdain to find himself often, marveled greatly at the concepts that divine love suggested to him. Among these the following is worthy of remembrance. He suddenly implored Cardinal Azzolino to supplicate Her Majesty the Queen to make an act of love to God on his behalf. He thought, as he said, that that great lady had a special language which God understood, while God used a language with her that she alone could understand.

The thought of that final step which was always present in his life had suggested to Bernini many years before his death the idea of asking Father Marchesi to assist him at his deathbed in all that he had to recall at that time. And since he feared that in the final extremity he might not be able to use his voice, which did in fact happen, he wished to be able to communicate with Father Marchesi by certain gestures and external motions which he had worked out to express the innermost feelings of his heart. It was a marvelous thing that, although Bernini could speak only brokenly during his illness as a result of the inflammation in his head, and that later, as a consequence of the new attack, he lost almost all power of speech, Father Marchesi always understood him. He gave such suitable replies to his reflections that they sufficed to lead him with admirable calm to his end.

Bernini's last breath was drawing near when he made a sign to Mattia de' Rossi and Giovan Battista Contini, his architectural assistants. Speaking as well as he was able, he said jokingly, while pointing to a precision instrument adapted to pulling heavy weights, that he was surprised that their invention would not serve to draw the catarrh from his throat. When his confessor asked about his soul's state of calm and whether he was fearful, he replied, "Father, I must render account to a Lord who in His goodness, does not count in farthings." Later because of the apoplexy his right arm and whole right side were paralyzed and he said, "It is good that this arm which has so wearied itself in life should rest a bit before death."

Meanwhile, Rome wept at her great loss. Bernini's house was filled by a continual flow of men of high rank and people of every station seeking news and wishing to visit him at the end. Her Majesty the Queen of Sweden, many cardinals, and ambassadors of princes came or sent messages at least twice a day. Finally, His Holiness sent his benediction, after which, at the beginning of the twenty-eighth day of the month of November of the year 1680, at about midnight, after fifteen days of illness, Bernini went to that other life. He was eighty-two years old less nine days.

In his will Bernini left His Holiness the Pope a large painting of Christ by his own hand. To Her Majesty the Queen of Sweden he left the beautiful marble image of the Saviour of which we have spoken; to the Most Eminent Cardinal Altieri, a marble bust-length portrait of Clement; to the Most Eminent Cardinal Azzolino, his most kind protector, a bust of Innocent X, his supporter. Not having anything else in marble he left Cardinal Rospigliosi a painting by his own hand. He most strictly enjoined that his beautiful statue of Truth be left in his own house. It is the only work by his chisel that remains the property of his children.

It would take too long to tell of the sorrow that such a loss brought to all Rome. I will only say that Her Majesty the Queen, whose sublime intellect knew through long experience the subtle gifts of so great a man, paid extraordinary tribute to him. It seemed to her that with Bernini's death the world had lost the one who had played a unique rôle in making our century glorious. On the day of Bernini's death the Pope sent a noble gift to that Queen by means of his privy chamberlain. The Queen asked the chamberlain what was being said in Rome concerning the estate left by Bernini. When she learned that it was worth about four hundred thousand scudi, she said, "I would be ashamed if he had served me and had left so little."

The pomp with which the body of our artist was borne to the church of S. Maria Maggiore where his family had their burial place, corresponded to the dignity of the deceased and the capabilities and love of his children, who ordered a most noble funeral and distributed both candles and alms on a grand scale. The talents and pens of the learned were exhausted in the composition of eulogies, sonnets, lyric poems, erudite verses in Latin, and the most ingenious vernacular poetry was written in praise of Bernini and publicly exhibited. All the Roman nobility and the ultramontane nobility then in the city gathered together. There was, in short, a crowd so numerous that it was necessary to postpone somewhat the time for the interment of the body. Bernini was buried in a lead coffin in the previously mentioned tomb commemorative of his name and of his person.

The Cavalier Giovan Lorenzo Bernini was a man of average stature with a somewhat dark complexion and black hair that turned white with age. His eye was spirited and lively with a piercing gaze under heavy eyebrows. His behavior was fiery; his speech made a most effective impression. When giving orders, he terrified by his gaze alone. He was much inclined to anger and quickly inflamed. To those who rebuked him for it, he would respond that the same fire that seared him more than others also impelled him to work harder than others who were not subject to such passions. This same natural fervor kept him in a state of poor health until the age of forty. Because of it he could not bear without injury the rays of the sun or even the reflection of the rays, which often gave him migraine. With increasing years this excessive heat lessened and he entered into a state of perfect health which he enjoyed until his last illness. His moderate eating habits helped maintain his good health. Ordinarily he allowed nothing to be prepared for him except a small dish of meat and a great quantity of fruit. He used to say in jest that this craving for fruit was the original sin of those born in Naples. With such an equable manner of life, Bernini kept himself so strong that he seemed to be tireless. Bernini said of himself that if he put together all the time he spent at meals and in sleep during his life, he thought all such inactivity would not come to a full month. Moreover, he never undertook any task that could be done by others. When not diverted by architectural projects, Bernini normally spent up to seven straight hours without resting when working in marble: a sustained effort that his young assistants could not maintain. If, sometimes, one of them tried to tear him away he would resist saying: "Let me stay here for I am enthralled." He remained, then, so steadfastly at his work that he seemed to be in ecstasy, and it appeared from his eyes that he wanted his spirit to issue forth to give life to the stone. Because of his intense concentration it was always necessary to have a young assistant on the scaffolding with him to prevent him from falling as he paid no attention when he moved about. The cardinals and princes who came to watch him work would seat themselves without a word and just as silently, so as not to distract him for a moment, make their departure. He proceeded in this manner for the entire working session and at the end he would be bathed in perspiration and, in his last years, very lowered in spirits. But because of his excellent constitution a little rest would restore him.

I would consider that I had done great wrong to Bernini's Christian piety if I attributed his accomplishments in art only to the natural strength of his constitution and his extraordinary merit. Bernini often thought and said to many persons that in the service of the Roman pontiffs and in the embellishment of St. Peter's he realized when his work was going well that this success came from the continuous support and help of the Prince of the Apostles to whom he was deeply devoted.

So far in my account of Bernini's works I have tried to follow an historical chronology. I would now like to touch in a general way on some other of his fine qualities, qualities either given him by nature or which, through long and diligent effort, were always and everywhere the inseparable companions of his deeds and had become second nature to him. First of all, we can with good reason affirm that Cavalier Bernini was most singular in the arts he pursued because he possessed in high measure skill in drawing. This is clearly demonstrated by the works he executed in sculpture, painting, and architecture and by the infinite number of his drawings of the human body which are to be found in almost all the most famous galleries in Italy and elsewhere. A group of these drawings merits a worthy place in the library of the Most Serene Cardinal Leopoldo de' Medici, of glorious memory. The Chigi family possesses many, and a great number of them were sent to France. In these drawings one notes a marvelous symmetry, a great sense of majesty, and a boldness of touch that is really a miracle. I would be at a loss to name a contemporary of Bernini who could be compared with him in that skill. A particular product of his boldness in drawing was his work in that sort of sketch we call caricature or "charged strokes," which for a joke distort in an uncomplimentary way the appearance of others, without taking away the likeness or grandeur if the subjects were, as often happened, princes. Such personages are inclined to be amused at such entertainment even when their own appearance is concerned and would pass around the drawings for other persons of high rank to see.

The opinion is widespread that Bernini was the first to attempt to unite architecture with sculpture and painting in such a manner that together they make a beautiful whole. This he accomplished by removing all repugnant uniformity of poses, breaking up the poses sometimes without violating good rules although he did not bind himself to the rules. His usual words on this subject were that those who do not sometimes go outside the rules never go beyond them. He thought, however, that those who were not skilled in both painting and sculpture should not put themselves to that test but should remain rooted in the good precepts of art. He knew from the beginning that his strong point was sculpture. Thus, although he felt a great inclination toward painting, he did not wish to devote himself to it altogether. We could say that his painting was merely diversion. Nevertheless, he made such great progress in that art that besides the paintings by his hand that are on public view, there are more than one hundred and fifty canvases, many owned by the most excellent Barberini and Chigi families and by Bernini's children. A very fine, lively self-portrait hangs in the famous gallery of self-portraits of great masters in the palace of the Most Serene Grand Duke of Tuscany.

Before Bernini's and our own day there was perhaps never anyone who manipulated marble with more facility and boldness. He gave his works a marvelous softness from which many great men who worked in Rome during his time learned. Although some censured the drapery of his figures as too complex and sharp, he felt this, on the contrary, to be a special indication of his skill. Through it he demonstrated that he had overcome the great difficulty of making the marble, so to say, flexible and of finding a way to combine painting and sculpture, something that had not been done by other artists. This was the case, he said, because they did not have the courage to render stones as obedient to the hand as if they were dough or wax. He said this without feelings of arrogance or presumption. He said it in order to explain himself and his work. In regard to the recognition of his own talent, he was always humble. He often said the more he worked, the more he recognized that he knew nothing. He held this belief so strongly that, although he never made a work without extraordinary love, once it was finished and he reflected upon its lack of the ultimate in beauty, he lost his affection for it and would look upon it no more. From this moderation in self-esteem Bernini developed great discretion in speaking of the works of others. He was accustomed to praise the good and to remain silent about what was lacking, and if there was nothing to praise, to invent ways of speaking without committing himself. Thus one time being brought by a cardinal to see a dome that the cardinal had had painted by one of his very favorite artists who had made a very bad job of it, when asked by the prelate in the presence of many masters of arts what he thought of it, Bernini observed it closely. He then said to the cardinal who, knowing little of art, expected to hear his painter praised, "Truly, the work speaks for itself," and he repeated the words energetically at least three times. Since one takes things in the way one wants to take them, the cardinal took Bernini's words as high praise, while the artists, looking into each others faces, laughed among themselves at the work. Bernini used to say that in order to give great praise to something it was not sufficient that it contain few errors but that it have great merits. To this judgment Cardinal Pallavicini, his intimate friend, added, "What you say of your art I say of mine, that the fact that there are insoluble arguments against something is not a sign of the falsity of the hypothesis, although it raises doubts, but whether there are solid and convincing reasons that prove the conclusion. Yet the philosopher Zeno used such arguments as proofs, and to this day that which he left has not been demolished."

Moreover, Bernini used to say that the worthy man was not he who made no errors, since that is an impossibility for those who do things, but he who made fewer errors than others; and that he, himself, had made more errors than any other artist, since he had made more works than any other. To one of his disciples who questioned him because he criticized beautiful things, he replied that there was no need to criticize ugly things, but rather the blameworthy aspects of beautiful things, thus seeking the perfect by the reflection of the good on the defects.

It is not easy to describe the love Bernini brought to his work. He said that, when he began work, it was for him like entering a pleasure garden.

There are many indications of that great esteem which he always aroused. As proof it will suffice to tell of the first time that Her Majesty the Queen of Sweden did him the honor of going to see him at work in his own house. Bernini received her in the heavy rough garment he was accustomed to wear when working in marble. Since it was what he wore for his art, he considered it to be the most worthy possible garment in which to receive that great lady. This beautiful subtlety was quickly perceived by the Queen's sublime genius. His action not only increased her concept of his spirit, but even led her, as a sign of her esteem for his art, to wish to touch the garment with her own hand.

Bernini had great knowledge and noble sentiments concerning the arts and those who professed them. To the general and habitual courtesy of those masters of art I here register my debt, as the fruits of this narrative come directly from them. Bernini wanted his students to love that which was most beautiful in nature. He said that the whole point of art consisted in knowing, recognizing, and finding it. He, therefore, did not accept the thesis of those who stated that Michelangelo and the ancient masters of Greece and Rome had added a certain grace to their work which is not found in the natural world. Nature knows how to give to every part its commensurate beauty, Bernini said, but one must know how to recognize it when the opportunity arises. In this regard he used to relate that in studying the Medici Venus he had at one time come to the same conclusion in observing her most graceful gesture. But since that time, having made profound studies of nature, he had clearly observed exactly the same graceful gesture on many occasions. He held that the story of the Venus that Zeuxis made was a fable: that is to say, the story that Zeuxis had made her from the most beautiful parts of many different girls, taking one part from one and another part from another. He said that the beautiful eyes of one woman do not go well with the beautiful face of another woman, and so it was with a beautiful mouth, and so on. I would say that this is absolutely true, since the various parts are not only beautiful in themselves but in their relationship to other parts. Thus the beautiful shaft of a column is praiseworthy for the proportions it has by itself, but if one adds a beautiful base and a fine capital that do not go with it, the column as a whole loses its beauty. This principle of Bernini's agrees with another of his concepts. He said that in making a portrait from life everything consisted in being able to recognize the unique qualities of individuality that nature gives to each person rather than the generality common to all. In choosing a particularity one must pick one that is beautiful rather than ugly. In order to achieve this end Bernini had a practice very different from the general run. He did not want the person he was drawing to remain immobile. Rather he wished him to move about and talk, since he said he then could see all his beauty and, as it were, capture it. He said that a person who poses, fixed and immobile, is never as much himself as he is when he is in motion, when those qualities which are his alone and not of a general nature appear. Such individuality gives a portrait its likeness. But a complete grasp of this is not a game for children.

In order to make the portrait of His Majesty the King of France Bernini first made many models. He removed all these models when he set to work in the presence of the King. When the monarch, wondering at his actions, asked why he did not want to make use of his work, Bernini replied that he had used models in order to introduce into his mind the features that he had to trace, but that once they had been envisaged and it was time to make them manifest, such models were no longer necessary: on the contrary, they impeded his purpose which was to conceive a likeness of reality rather than a likeness of the models. Since we are speaking of that great King, I will repeat what Bernini used to say of him, that he never knew a mind as able as the King's to adapt itself to the cognition of beauty.

He used to say that all the delight of our senses is in imitation. As an example of this he pointed out the great enjoyment that comes from seeing a fine painting of a rancid and loathsome old woman, who in living and breathing flesh would nauseate and offend us.

In his works, whether large or small, Bernini strove with everything in him to make resplendent all the conceptual beauty inherent in whatever he was working on. He said that he was accustomed to putting in no less study and application in designing an oil lamp than in designing a very noble edifice. In preparing his works he would consider one thing at a time. He gave this procedure as a precept to his disciples, that is to say, first comes the concept, then reflection on the arrangement of the parts, and finally giving the perfection of grace and sensitivity to them. As an example he cited the orator who first conceives, then orders, elaborates, and embellishes. He said that each of these operations demanded the whole man and that to do more than one thing at a time was impossible.

He placed the most famous painters in the following order:

The first and most important he said was Raphael whom he called a bottomless vessel that collected waters from all the springs; that is to say, Raphael possessed the most perfect aspects of all the others together. After him he put Correggio, then Titian, and finally Annibale Carracci. He gave first place of excellence among Raphael's works to the rooms of Pope Paul that he painted and the rooms of Peace and the beautiful portrait of Bindo Altoviti, which is owned by Monsignor Antonio Altoviti, a most noble Florentine cavalier, who was auditor to the Most Eminent Cardinal Alderano Cibò and is now secretary of the Council. Bernini said that Guido Reni had a style enriched by such fine concepts that his paintings delight not only skilled artists but also the uneducated.

He used particularly beautiful aphorisms regarding nobility or pre-eminence in the arts. Bernini declared that painting was superior to sculpture, since sculpture shows that which exists with more dimensions while painting shows that which does not exist, that is, it shows relief where there is no relief and gives an effect of distance where there is none. However, there is a certain greater difficulty in executing a likeness in sculpture and, as proof, Bernini pointed to the fact that a man who loses his color no longer looks like himself, whereas sculpture is able to create a likeness in white marble.

The great art in bas-relief, he said, was in making things appear in relief that are not in relief. In speaking of high-relief, particularly those in Alexander's apartment, he used to say that they were of little technical skill since they are almost completely in the round, and are what they appear to be, rather than appearing to be what they are not. He said that among the works of antiquity, the Laocoön and the Pasquin contain, in themselves, all the best of art, since one sees in them all that is most perfect reproduced without the affectation of art. The most beautiful statues existing in Rome, he said, were the Belvedere Torso and the Laocoön, of those still whole: the Laocoön for its emotional content, particularly for the understanding it displays in that leg, which already being affected by the poison seems to be numb. Bernini, however, said that the Torso and the Pasquin seemed to him more perfect stylistically than the Laocoön, but that the Laocoön was whole while the others were not. He said the difference between the Pasquin and the Torso is almost imperceptible and could not be perceived except by a great man, but that such a man would find the Pasquin to be rather better. Bernini was the first in Rome to place the Pasquin highest. He told of one time being asked by someone from beyond the Alps which was the most beautiful statue in Rome, and that when he responded, the Pasquin, the foreigner thought he was joking, so he went with him to prove it.

Bernini had splendid precepts concerning architecture: first of all he said the highest merit lay not in making beautiful and commodious buildings, but in being able to make do with little, to make beautiful things out of the inadequate and ill-adapted, to make use of a defect in such a way that if it had not existed one would have to invent it. Many of his works attest that his skill came up to that level. It is seen, especially, in Urban VIII's coat of arms in the Church of Aracoeli. There, since the logical space to place the emblem was occupied by a large window, he colored the glass blue and on it represented the three bees as if flying through the air, and above he placed the triple crown. He proceeded in a similar way in the tomb of Alexander VII and in the placement of the cathedra, where the window was turned from an impediment into an asset: around it he represented a Vision of Glory, and in the very center of the glass, as if in place of the inaccessible light, he portrayed the Holy Spirit in the form of a dove which brings the whole work to a consummation. He put such ideas in practice more than once in the designing of fountains. The fountain for Cardinal Antonio Barberini at Bastioni is a fine example. Since there was very little water and very thin jets, he represented a woman who, having washed her hair, squeezes it to produce a thin spray of water which satisfies both the needs of the fountain and the action of the figure. Though this is a concept that had been used earlier by another artist for a fountain for the Most Serene Grand Duke of Tuscany, we can believe it was also reborn in Bernini's charming fancy. In another fountain made for the Duke Girolamo Mattei for his famous villa at the Navicella he wished to do something great and majestic, but the water would only rise a little. He made a representation of Mount Olympus, on which he placed the figure of a flying eagle, an emblem of the Mattei, which also makes an effective reference to the mountain. He placed clouds midway up the mountain, since they could not rise to the summit of Olympus, and from these clouds rain fell. Another of his precepts should be brought forth since we are speaking of fountains. It is that since fountains are made for the enjoyment of water, then the water should always be made to fall so that it can be seen. It was with such a precept in mind, I believe, that in his restoration of the bridge of Sant'Angelo by order of Clement IX, he had the side walls lowered so that the water could better be enjoyed. The eye then may see with double pleasure from the banks of the river the flow of water as well as the bridge above, ornamented with angels that allude to its ancient name.

Bernini's ingenuity did not stop at matters of art. He brought forth noble concepts, acute sayings, and witty pleasantries on every occasion. Although I do not think it necessary to record many of them, but since I am convinced it would be less than fitting to remain completely silent, I shall note some of them. The Cavalier had made the bronze crucifix of which we spoke elsewhere for His Majesty the King of Spain, and he made a similar one for himself. While he was in France, he ordered his family to present his crucifix to Cardinal Pallavicini. Later the same Cardinal, when speaking to Bernini, could not find words enough to praise the beauty of the crucifix. Bernini responded: "I will say to Your Eminence what I said in France to Her Majesty the Queen when she praised me so highly for my portrait of the King, her husband.

Your Majesty praises the copy so much because she is in love with the original." While Bernini was still in the service of Louis, the monarch appeared somewhat hesitant in having him see Versailles where there are many beautiful, tiny things. Finally, one morning finding Bernini there he asked him his opinion of it. "Sire," he replied, "I believed that Your Majesty was great in great things, I now know that you are great in little things as well." Asked in the presence of many French ladies which were the most beautiful, Italian or French women, he responded, "All are very beautiful, with this difference, however: under the skin of Italian women runs blood and under that of French women, milk." When someone said to him that a certain artist who had executed a fine work in painting had not done a great thing since he had received, so people said, Bernini's guidance (which was not true), he said, "Sad is the house that needs props." One time someone, I don't know who, said to him that a certain person who had been his assistant was a very able architect. He replied, "You are quite right, because he cuts corners." To a great prelate who was saying that he could not endure the aforementioned architect's inordinate desire to break the rules of the good designer and modeler that he was, who had in some cases so far missed the mark in his works that some of them seemed to draw from the Gothic style rather than from the good modern or antique mode, Bernini responded, "What you are saying, sir, is very pertinent, but I think it is better to be a bad Catholic than a good heretic." Now let us pass on to other qualities of Bernini.

He who pointed out that poetry is painting that speaks and, conversely, that painting is a kind of mute poetry spoke well. But if such a description fits poetry in general, it is much more suited to that kind of poetry called dramatic or illustrative. In such poetry, as in a beautiful historical painting, we note various persons of diverse ages, conditions, and customs, each with an individuality of appearance and action, with admirably distributed colors which form, as do the voices of a well-balanced choir, a beautiful and marvelous composition. Therefore, it is not surprising at all that a man of Bernini's excellence in the three arts, whose common source is drawing, also possessed in high measure the fine gift of composing excellent and most ingenious theatrical productions since it derives from the same genius and is the fruit of the same vitality and spirit. Bernini was, then, outstanding in dramatic actions and in composing plays. He put on many productions which were highly applauded for their scope and creativity during the time of Urban VIII and Innocent X. He created most admirably all the parts both serious and comic in all the various styles that up to his time had been represented on the stage. He enriched them further with such ideas that the learned who heard them attributed some to Terence, others to Plautus and similar authors that Bernini had never read. He created them all by the force of his genius. Sometimes it took an entire month for Bernini to act out all the parts himself in order to instruct the others and then to adapt the part for each individual. The keenness of the witticisms, the bizarreness of the devices through which he derided abuses and struck at bad behavior were such that whole books could be made of them, not without delight to those who might wish to read them. But I leave all of them for someone better. It was, nevertheless, wonderful to see that those who were the butt of his witticisms and mockeries, who for the most part were present at the performances, never took offense. Bernini's ability to blend his talents in the arts for the invention of stage machinery has never been equalled in my opinion. They say that in the celebrated spectacle *The Inundation of the Tiber* he made it appear that a great mass of water advanced from far away little by little breaking through the dikes. When the water broke through the last dike facing the audience, it flowed forward with such a rush and spread so much terror among the spectators that there was no one, not even among the most knowledgeable, who did not quickly get up to leave in fear of an actual flood. Then, suddenly, with the opening of a sluice gate, all the water was drained away.

Another time he made it appear that by a casual unforeseen accident the theatre caught fire. Bernini represented a carnival carriage, behind which some servants with torches walked. The person whose job it was to perpetrate the trick repeatedly brushed his torch against the stage set as happened sometimes. It was as if he wanted to spread the flames above the wall partitions. Those who did not know the game cried out loudly for him to stop so that he would not set fire to the scenery. Scarcely had fear been engendered in the audience by the action and the outcry, when the whole set was seen burning with artificial flames. There was such terror among the spectators that it was necessary to reveal the trick to keep them from fleeing. Afterward there was another noble and beautiful scene.

Once he composed two prologues for a spectacle to be performed in two theatres, one opposite the other, so that the people could hear the play in one theatre as well as in the other. The spectators in the regular theatre, who were the most important and famous, saw themselves re-created in effigy by masks in the other theatre in a manner so lifelike that they were amazed. One of the prologues faced outward, while the other was reversed, as the parts were played. It was delightful to see the departure of the people—in carriages, on foot, and on horseback—at the conclusion.

The fame of the play *La Fiera,* produced for Cardinal Antonio Barberini during the reign of Urban VIII, will live forever. There was everything in it that one is accustomed to seeing in such gatherings. The same is true of the spectacle *La Marina* which was done with a new invention and that of the *Palazzo d'Atlante e d'Astolfo* which astonished the age.

It was Bernini who first invented that beautiful stage machine for representing the rising of the sun. It was so much talked about that Louis XIII, the French King of glorious memory, asked him for a model of it. Bernini sent it to him with careful instructions, at the end of which he wrote these words, "It will work when I send you my head and hands." He said he had a fine idea for a play in which all the errors that come from running the stage machinery would be revealed along with their corrections, and still another not yet presented, for giving the ladies away on the stage. He disapproved of horses or other real creatures appearing on stage, saying that art consists in everything being simulated although seeming to be real.

More could be said here which for the sake of brevity is passed over. I will close this section with Cardinal Pallavicini's familiar remark that Cavalier Bernini was not only the best sculptor and architect of his century but, to put it simply, the greatest man as well. A great theologian, he said, or a great captain or great orator might have been valued more highly, as the present century thinks such professions either more noble or more necessary. But there was no theologian who had advanced as far in his profession during that period as Bernini had advanced in his.

It is not surprising, then, that one can say that Bernini was always highly esteemed and even revered by the great. He was so generously remunerated that it seems to be a certainty that there was no one else in recent centuries, no matter what his excellence, whose works were so richly rewarded. We have spoken in previous accounts of the tributes he received from the great: of the visits of pontiffs, of that of Her Majesty the Queen of Sweden, and of many cardinals. We will add that Bernini constantly received Italian and ultramontane princes who were drawn to his house by the desire to see him work. Cardinal Maffeo Barberini (later Urban VIII), Cardinal Fabio Chigi (later Alexander VII), the Cardinals Antonio Barberini, Rapaccioli, Chigi, and Rinaldo d'Este visited him constantly. The last named esteemed so greatly even a line from Bernini's hand that when he took him to Tivoli to see if the design of a fountain for his famous garden had been well executed, he made him a gift of a ring with five diamonds for a slight retouching of certain stuccos; and afterwards Cardinal d'Este rewarded him with a silver basin of like value. His Holiness Innocent XI, the reigning pontiff, showed how highly he valued

Bernini when he cut the expenses and appropriations for the palace extensively; in words filled with love and great esteem he ordered that Bernini's allowance be left intact.

Bernini had many followers in the arts of painting, sculpture, and architecture, and we shall here note some of the more prominent. First place must go to Luigi di Pietro Bernini, blood brother of the Cavalier, a good sculptor, a better architect, and an excellent mathematician. He worked for a time at sculpture. In Rome he carved the putto on the right hand side of the tomb of Countess Matilda of Tuscany, whose statue, except for the head which was the work of Giovan Lorenzo, he carved. He worked in St. Peter's in the area of the choir and in the Chapel of the Most Holy Sacrament. He made the four marble figures of Fame which bear the arms of Innocent X; the bas-relief over the statue of St. Helena, where the relics are shown; the two putti of the first chapel on the left of the entrance of St. Peter's where the cathedra had been placed earlier; and another two in the Barberini Chapel. His work is also seen in S. Andrea della Valle and elsewhere. Later Luigi Bernini dedicated himself to civil architecture, mathematics, mechanics, and, especially, to speculation concerning the forces and measurement of enclosed waters. He advanced so much in each of these fine disciplines that later on the Cavalier, his brother, always discussed his most difficult problems with him. Among these were the erection of the obelisk in Piazza Navona and the Scala Regia. And although Luigi's position as superintendent of the construction of the Apostolic Palaces was under the direction of Giovan Lorenzo he was often allowed to work on his own, since the architect was sure that his brother would not err. Luigi contrived that fine scaffold, ninety palmi high, to facilitate work in the upper parts of St. Peter's. We see it being pulled here and there in the great church with a marvelous movement aided by steering devices for each movable part. It completely supplanted the old structure which ground down the floors so much when it was moved that the cost of the damage every year was enormous.

The ability to move the great organ of St. Peter's from place to place—until then the work of twenty men—without dismantling it was his discovery as was the device for pulling as many as fourteen cartloads of travertine with great ease. Also his was that instrument consisting of a great jib seventy palmi high to which were joined two others from each of which hung two iron tackles six and a half palmi long, cast in one piece and containing six metal disks, three on each side. With this machine, never before seen or used, all the stones of the colonnades and portico of St. Peter's were put in place. But the most wonderful of all his inventions was the iron steelyard twenty palmi long that he contrived solely in order to weigh the colossal bronze statues of the cathedra of St. Peter's. The steelyard, through the action of a smaller balance with a capacity of no more than ten pounds attached to the top to establish the weight, was capable of weighing up to thirty-six thousand pounds. This invention, which was highly applauded by artists and everyone, is today kept in the storerooms of the Fabbrica of the basilica. This artist's skilled hand and talent produced many other fine inventions during the sixty-nine prosperous years of his life.

Bernini's most beloved assistant was Mattia de' Rossi, a Roman. He was the son of Marcantonio de' Rossi, a good architect of his time. The charm of manner, animation, knowledge, and the other fine qualities of this man are such and so well known in Rome that now one need only say his name to call forth the greatest praise. We must add that for the space of twenty-five years he worked directly with the master, and always followed him with filial love until he died. De' Rossi now demonstrates the talents of his vital spirit in his position as superintendent of the Fabbrica of St. Peter's and, moreover, fills the post of architect of St. Peter's, an office formerly held by his master, Cavalier Bernini, as we related elsewhere.

Francesco Mochi, who made the statue of St. Veronica in one of the crossing piers of St. Peter's, studied with Bernini. It is said, however, that later he retained little memory of the kindness that he received from the master. Also with Bernini was Franceso Duquesnoy, called the Fleming, who took the marvelous delicacy found in his work from Bernini. Duquesnoy greatly distinguished himself in making figures of small children and others. He modeled excellently in wax and cloth. Giovan Pietro Bellori has written of him in his usual erudite fashion in his book on modern painters, sculptors, and architects. Cavalier Borromini spent many years in the house of our artist learning the art of architecture. He became a very experienced master. However, following his own caprice, he was inclined to use too much originality in the ornamentation of buildings, sometimes venturing too far from the rule and approaching the Gothic manner.

Among Bernini's disciples are Cavalier Carlo Fontana and Giovan Battista Contini, architects; Giuliano Finelli, famous in sculpture; and Lazzero Morelli of Ascoli Piceno who worked as a sculptor in Rome. Giulio Cesare, who, as we mentioned earlier, went to Paris with Bernini, served and aided him until his death. Others include Jacopo Antonio Fancelli; Stefano Speranza; Andrea Bolgi, who carved the figure of St. Helena in St. Peter's; Gio. Antonio Mari; and, finally, Niccolò Sale, a Frenchman, who made the putti and medallions in St. Peter's and some bas-reliefs for the Raimondi Chapel in S. Pietro in Montorio. Sale entered the service of the Cavalier in the capacity of manager of household expenses. But being much inclined toward sculpture, he started to study on his own and later on to work in his own studio, until he had acquired such a good style that he was given the opportunity to make many works. He was a man of Christian habits and was most exemplary, but he was one of those persons who believe that everyone is the same as he. He became too trusting and consigned two thousand scudi to a certain man to deliver to a sister he had living in the country. Whether because of the man's unexpected death or because he was robbed or some other misfortune befell him, or whether he actually absconded to enjoy the money elsewhere, the unfortunate Sale never received confirmation that the money reached the intended recipient. This caused him such great grief that he died of it. Then there were many artists who did not receive their instruction from Bernini and had already established themselves as masters of art who worked with him and perfected themselves. Among these were Francesco Baratta, Ercole Ferrata, and Antonio Raggi, called the Lombard, who began his studies with Algardi and was the artist who made the figure of the Danube in the fountain at Piazza Navona.

But now it is time to satisfy the debt that a little earlier I contracted with my readers and give exact and clear information regarding the empty clamorings that broke out during Bernini's last years and continued for some months after his death. I do this so the world may know on what little basis stupid people sometimes act. They ordinarily have in their apprehension and opinions a proclivity for encouraging bad taste in others and for counseling ignorance; therefore such people act quickly, willingly point out, and most openly resolve to think, to believe, and to publish every inappropriate, even impossible occurrence, provided it contains something highly injurious to the well-being and happiness of others or something which—though false—has the appearance of truth.

We know then that in the year of 1680 in the month of April in the city of Rome some persons turned their attention to a certain old crack in the cupola of St. Peter's that had always been visible to everyone. The one who saw it then for the first time must have been a man of such low intelligence that either by standing there and looking up at it or by pointing it out to others as something new, he caused it to be talked about by a few people and then by many and then by so many that in a brief time all Rome had the idea that the dome had begun to move and that this movement, with the passage of time, would weaken the building and put it in danger of collapse. But ordinarily it is the practice in such discussions and in the spreading of such news by those who are hasty but do not wish to seem so, to produce some evidence in the area where their gossip does not appear to be based on any clear reason. Therefore, they began investigating the crack with all their might. As a result not much time passed before everyone in Rome started to say that the reason for the crack and the danger feared consequent to it was the embellishment carried out in St. Peter's after Bernini's plans by the order of Urban VIII. They saw very clear evidence of this when they observed the incisions which they said were made in the walls of the four piers or giant pillars on which the four large arches that hold up the dome rest—they said these incisions were cut to make the four niches on the ground level of the church where today we see the four marble colossi: SS. Andrew, Longinus, Helena, and Veronica—and also the incisions for the four upper niches where the sacred relics are kept and other incisions made in the same walls for the four spiral staircases which lead from the floor of the church to the upper niches.

These completely hollow, vulgar ideas were so alive and, indeed, so forceful that they succeeded in arousing the prudent diligence of that person who had charge of the maintenance of St. Peter's. He personally arranged that which was deemed practical in such a case: after thoroughly checking the substance of the gossip against the facts, he determined to issue a report. This he did. It was his judgment that the movement of the dome had no other cause than the afore-mentioned incisions and alterations in the piers. But, truthfully, before making such a report with such fine frankness that person might have taken the time to look at and study the old plans of Bramante Lazzeri, who in the pontificate of Julius II began to build the great basilica; the plan that Baldassare Peruzzi made during the same pontificate after Bramante's death; the plan that Antonio da Sangallo made during the pontificate of Paul III; the plan made by the great Michelangelo; and, finally, the plan made under Paul V by Carlo Maderno who built the addition to the church by extending the base of the cross. In all of these plans he would have seen the niches in the piers in exactly the same places and positions where they are to be seen today. And he would have been able to discern in those plans facts that would have saved him from such a badly conceived idea.

But he who follows the chatter of vulgar persons, those used to constructing castles without foundations and buildings in the air which time does not destroy but which vanish like smoke in the wind (as today we find to have happened with all that they said)—such a one has little need of designs and plans.

Therefore, in my opinion that report, so much in accordance with the general clamor, gave just cause for His Holiness Innocent XI, the reigning pontiff, prudently to command through Monsignor Giannuzzi, keeper and secretary of St. Peter's, that Mattia de' Rossi apply himself diligently to discover what was the truth and right of the whole matter. This Rossi did with great love and labor, poring over the site inside and out, studying the most minute details. Finally, he gave his judgment, and from it I have drawn all that I shall discuss.

According to the only limitations of the first orders given to Rossi, Giannuzzi's services were not to be used. His Holiness had, himself, possibly been impelled to this action because he already had a report from him. He ordered that two other architects be brought in to fill his posts. They were Carlo Fontana and Giovanni Antonio de' Rossi. Mattia arranged that they should see everything necessary at the site as well as all the old and new designs and plans. He communicated to them his own studies. The many visits to the sites and the conferences, the perusal of the report he had already made, were all punctually carried out by Mattia. In the end their judgment consisted of a complete rejection of the report by the person first summoned to the task and complete agreement with Mattia's report, which was based on such truth and clarity of reasoning that no more could be wished. I shall now undertake to present some of this material.

In order for the reader to understand these matters better, it would be useful if first of all he would familiarize himself with the plan of the whole church of St. Peter's which I have deliberately placed first among the drawings shown later in this work. The reader should also study the plan of the dome itself which I have placed second (Figs. 1 and 2). You will observe that there are four ground piers in this church that support the four great arches on which the dome rests, that is to say, there are two ground piers in the middle of the nave and another two forming the arms of the crossing. All together they circumscribe an octagonal space. These ground piers are so vast that the surfaces, measured in their essentials, without taking into account the projections of the pilasters, have a circumference of no less than three hundred and twenty palmi. The four niches are on the four shortest sides of these piers as the second drawing shows (Fig. 2). Above each of these great arches, at a level with the paired columns of the drum, are placed two piers with their pilasters and projections as shown in B of Fig. 2. The other two piers are set over each of the four pendentives which rise from between the haunches of the great arches as is shown in G. In its circumference, because of being diametric to the wall of the dome it extends about seventeen palmi from the columns of the ground pier to the columns of the drum. The drum, no matter how much the two piers indicated in G extend themselves, is certainly not placed over the ground piers. Only the two projections of the domical pier by the paired columns of the drum rest there, and they are placed over the strong point of the niche. Between these projections there is an open space through which anyone who comes to see this building can walk. Directly above the same niche, in the circulation passageway of the drum between the domical piers, and at the center of each of the pendentives is a large window.

Granting that this great dome was built in the indicated fashion and form and that the architect who planned it wished to leave a straight passageway or corridor in the place where the front of the niche begins in each of the aforesaid piers, such a passageway to cross in a diagonal line in alignment with the face of the same niche and to be of a height proportionate to its width with a good arch forming a vault for the whole width, and that such passageway or corridor be unbroken also and of the same width as the niche, there is not and never will be anyone in this world with the slightest understanding of these arts who could state that such a passageway could ever have been able to give any occasion for any movement in the dome, as such movement would be arrested by the two solid volumes of the wall, which are doubled and redoubled in relation to the width of the void.

Accepting this as true—and it is indeed very true—how is it possible ever to concede that the niche alone could weaken the whole structure and give the dome occasion to move? It is an unquestioned principle of good architects that if in the course of time a building makes some movement, then such movement always occurs in the weakest part. Therefore, there can never be any doubt that if the niche incisions had been the cause of the weakening of the ground piers sustaining the dome, then the precise place in the pier where the niche is located would show the first signs of movement, as in such an eventuality it would be deemed the weakest part. Nor would it have ended there, as the first movement would have been followed by other movements in the dome. However, we find, on the contrary, that this part of the pier is secure, intact and in alignment. Thus it follows that the idea of those who wished to say that the supposed movement of the dome resulted from the niche incisions would be false, empty, and unfounded in reason. Indeed, on the assumption that the building was constructed in the manner indicated and as the plans demonstrate it to have been, we may add that, if the architect who planned it wanted to make four large windows in a form similar to the four tondi of the pendentives where we see the four mosaics of the Evangelists, shown in the sectional elevations of the interior of St. Peter's (Fig. 4), any time during the period when they were fabricating the great arches, if he made use of good arches in such a manner that they would provide a counterthrust against the four principal arches of the church, no one doubts in terms of good and solid architecture that they would have had great strength and stability and that they would not have been able to provoke any movement. He would not have placed, moreover, any wall over the tondi other than one of the height of the base of the drum, since there were next repeated window openings between the columns, as we see in the plan. There was, as well, the void of the oculus in the middle of the base of the lantern on a plumb line between the domical piers that rest on the dome pendentives.

And who does not know that in making a dome the greatest task lies in placing it on the four arches which form the nave and crossing of the church. Under these same arches there is no wall of any sort but rather open space. Yet the arches stand straight and the structure is solid. Therefore, it can be affirmed as fact that neither the portals nor the niches beneath wherein we see the incisions in the piers could have ever of themselves caused any movement of the dome, weakening the area above the four pendentives which form enclosures and abutments between the one and the other of the arches. This is true for other reasons as well, which without my dwelling upon them further, will be well known to those truly expert in art.

But those who look upon a building only as something already made cannot understand or know how it is held up and are incapable as well of understanding how it may fall. Therefore, it is not surprising that some have come forth with ideas so strange and so contrary to good rules of art. It would seem that the reasons that have been pointed out, pertaining only to the constitution of the building, would be sufficient to expose the baselessness of the vulgar gossip. But since it is my intention to reduce the whole matter to a state of perfect clarity and to make it understandable to the learned and the ignorant alike, it is necessary that I go somewhat further.

Thus I say that these whisperings, among the common people

Giovan Lorenzo Bernini.
Engraving after painting by G. B. Gaulli

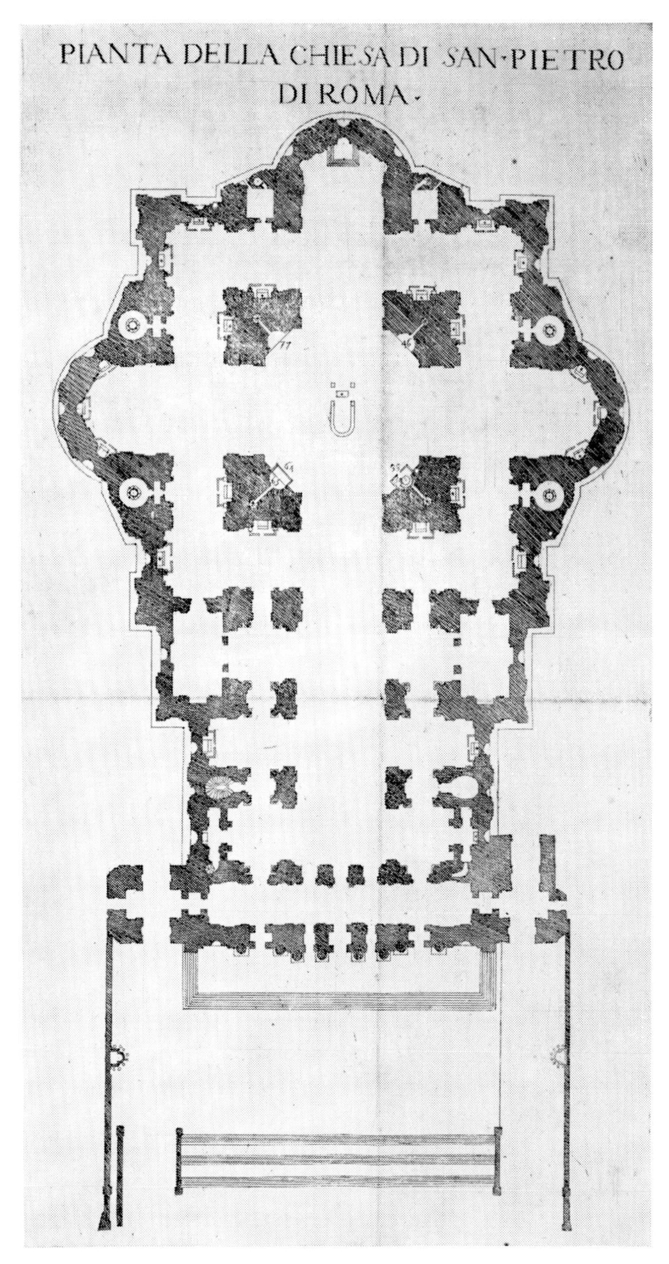

Fig. 1.
Plan of St. Peter's, Rome

A : Diametro è uano del Tamburo della Cuppola nella parte di dentro della Chiesa di palmi 190 3/4 misurato nel suo uiuo

B : N.º 08 pilastroni del Tamburo della Cuppolla, che posano sopra li quattro arconi della Chiesa; due della naue di mezo, è due delli bracci, che fanno Croce, composti di due pillastri per ciascheduno nella parte di dentro è suoi resalti per di fuori doue sono li uani delle porte, che ui si passa sotto è due Colōñe per ciascheduno

C : Dimostra li quattro piloni doue impostano li quattro arconi che sustenghono la Cuppola

D : le quattro nicchie doue sono le quattro statue al piano della Chiesa et altre quattro nichie di sopra dette delle Reliquie

E : li quattro pozi antichi di diametro palmi 7 doue sono le quattro Scale lumache, con Scalini di Tra.no tre de quali principiano dal pauimento della Chiesa è termineno al piano del nichie è L altro doue è il uolto santo seguita sino incima la fabrica al piano dell Apostoli

F : Passi è corridori antichi che conducono dalle Scale alle Nichie longhi l'uno p.mi 23 largh l'uno p.mi 4

G : N.º 8 pilastroni che posano sopra li quattro petti che fanno rifianchi è serragli alli quattro Arconi principali che sustengono la Cuppola

Palmi 200 — 50 — 100 — 150 — 200 Romani

Fig. 2.
Plan of the drum superimposed on a plan of the piers at the crossing of St. Peter's

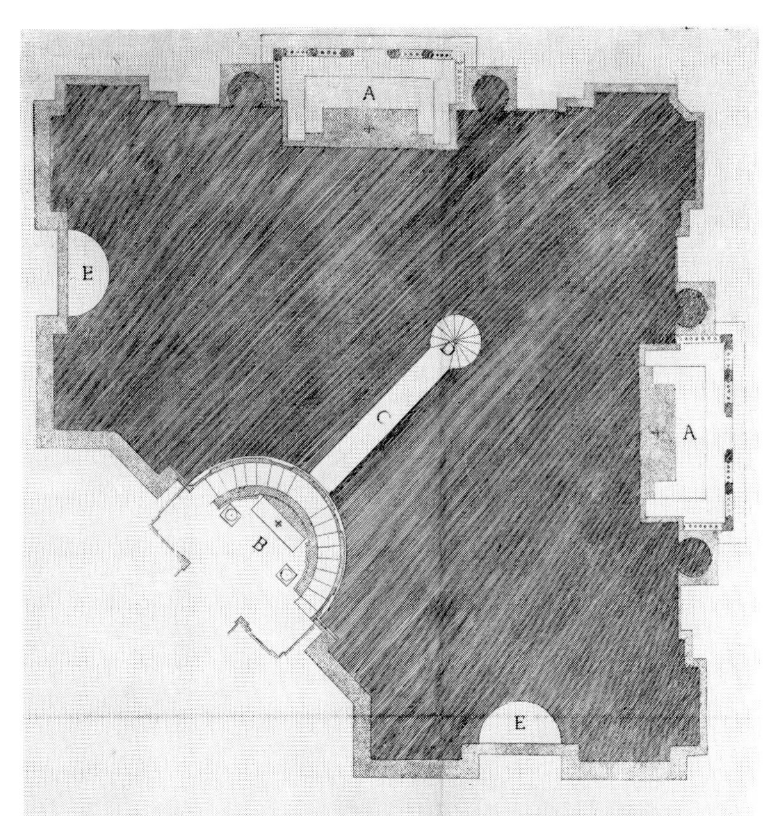

Disegnio di uno delli quattro Pilastroni doue impostano li quattro Arconi che sustengono la Cuppola della Chiesa di S. Pietro, dal quale si uede la sua uastità, e grandezza hauendo di giro nella sua superficie misurata nell' uiuo senza l'aggetti di pilastri palmi 320

A: Due Cappelle che sono in detto Pilastrone con Balustrata attorno ciascheduna di esse
B. Nicchia doue è la Veronica con Scala, che scende alla Confessione, e Grotte
C: Corridore che da detta Nicchia uà alla Scala lumaca, che salle alla Nicchia di sopra dell' Volto Santo, longo detto Corridore palmi 23 largno palmi 4
D: Scala lumaca, che dal' piano della Chiesa Salle alla Nicchia superiore dell Volto Santo; il diametro della quale sono palmi sette
E: Due Nicchie in detto Pilastrone lassate per situarui Statue &c

Palmi 60 — 5 — 10 — 20 — 30 — 40 — 50 — 60 Romani

Fig. 3.
The plan of one of the crossing piers, St. Peter's

Fig. 4.
Sectional drawing of dome and crossing piers, St. Peter's

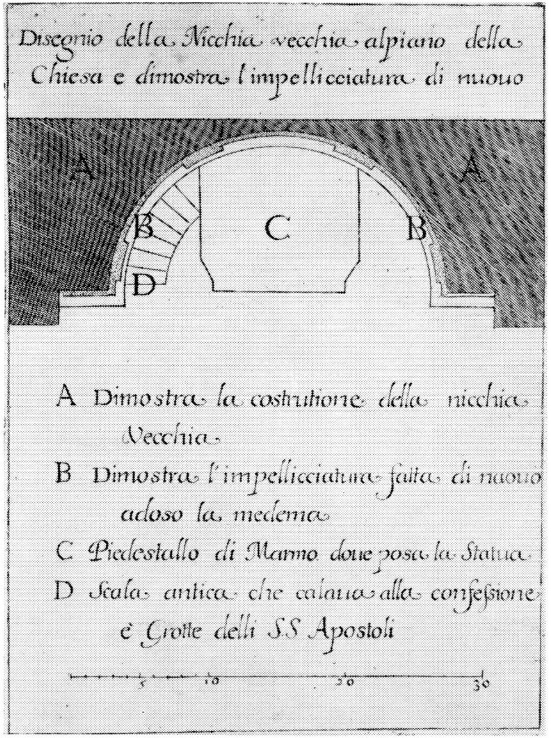

Fig. 5.
Plan of the lower niche in a crossing pier of St. Peter's, showing the new resurfacing

Fig. 6.
Plan of the upper niche in a crossing pier of St. Peter's

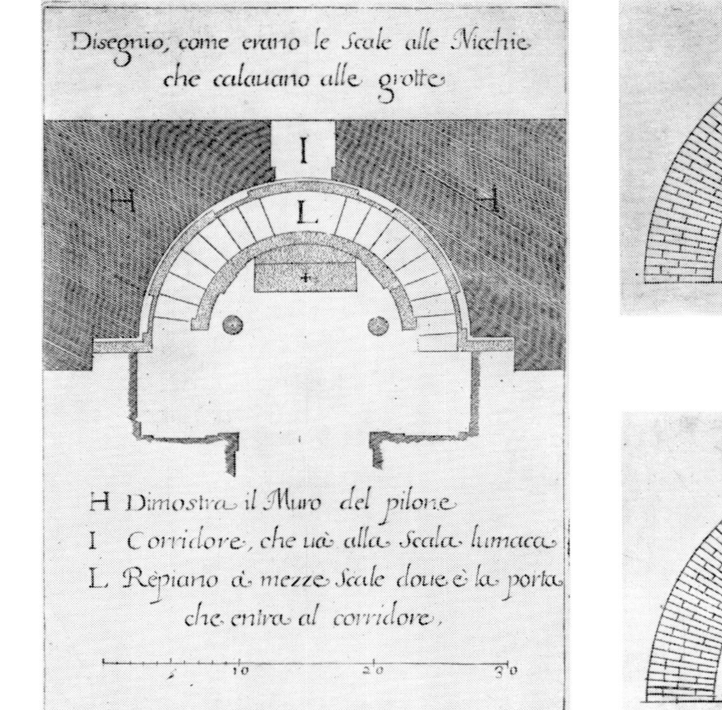

Fig. 7.
Plan of the lower niche in a crossing pier of St. Peter's, showing stairs leading to crypt

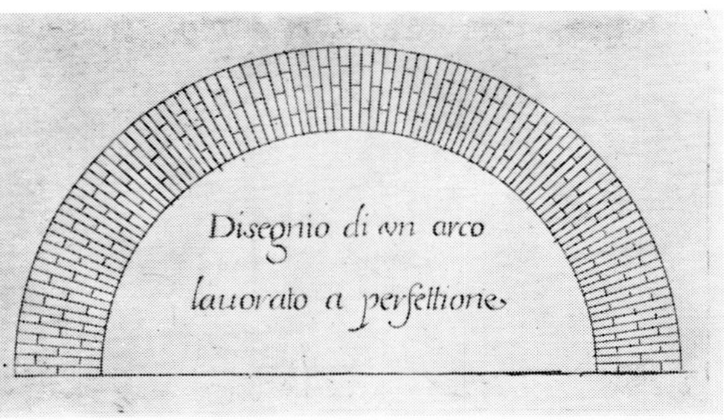

Fig. 8.
Plan of a well-made arch

Fig. 9.
Plan of a badly made arch

as well as among artists of little experience, were baseless not only because they were contrary to the sound reasons of the discipline but also because they were founded on completely false premises.

It is not true that the incisions for the niches in the piers that carry the dome were the work of Bernini. Rather they were the work of the celebrated architects of whom we made mention at the beginning of this discussion. Let us look at the plan that Maderno had printed and at the legend where the parts illustrated are noted. There, in sequence, we read:

No. 33. Niche containing the white marble column on which, according to ancient tradition, Our Lord Jesus Christ often leaned when he preached to the people in the Temple of Solomon, and through which people possessed are seen miraculously cured.

No. 46. Niche at the ground level of the church, and above, where the head of the glorious St. Andrew the Apostle is kept.

No. 64. Niche at the ground level of the church for the tomb of Paul III.

No. 77. Niche at the ground level of the church and another above where the Most Holy Sudarium and the Lance which opened the side of Our Lord Jesus Christ are with great veneration preserved.

In this regard see also Abramo Bzovio's *Life of Paul V*, translated by Bartolommei.

There is no doubt that Cavalier Bernini, by order of Urban VIII, did some work in St. Peter's in and about the niches on the ground level of the church and on the upper level. However, this work was to enlarge the circumference surfaces of the lower niches, to add the marble facings of the niches, and to provide the four bases of white marble on which the four colossi stand. For greater clarity the drawing and plan are reproduced in Fig. 5 at the end.

The work in the four upper niches is evident from the appearance of the place. Nevertheless, we show the plan in Fig. 6. In substance, the work consisted in increasing the adornment of the interior which had been made earlier in each of these same niches where the eight columns of white marble from Solomon's temple with their bases of similar marble are located. Bas-reliefs were added above and decorations in mosaic work of multicolored stones in the background. Bernini also brought forward the openings or, as we say, the niche cavities that already were there. Thus, we see that the niches were not made deeper or dug out further than they were already but were, rather, filled in. In this regard, look at the design of the previously mentioned plan. It can be seen that the circumference and concavity of the old niches above were in direct alignment with the niches below. This is amply demonstrated by the space still remaining today between the old and the new niches. This space was left with wise foresight by the architect so that the dampness of the marbles which ordinarily transmit air into the walls would not damage them, and they would stay drier.

They said, moreover, that the walls of the four piers were cut into in order to make the four spiral staircases which go from the floor of the church to the four upper niches. But in that same plan there definitely are provisions for the four stairways. Therefore, we can clearly see that the four shafts were left by the architects with the sole intention of placing the four spiral staircases there. We also know for a certainty that there were four upper niches there, which were to serve for the placement of relics or organs or other similar things. We also know that the Sacred Sudarium was displayed from one of these niches. According to Giovanni Severano, it was placed there by Paul V as far back as January 29, 1605. Bzovio clearly states that Paul placed the Holy Lance of Our Lord in a high place, where it is now seen. Who, then, would wish to think that men of such high merit, as were the architects who worked on St. Peter's during those times, would not have provided some means of ascent to those high and most worthy places other than a rope or step ladder to be attached to or leaned against the piers in the interior of the church? It must then be said that the shafts left in those walls could serve no other purpose than to accommodate the spiral stairs. And who does not know that to one of those upper niches, specifically the one that contains the Sacred Sudarium, one ascends by means of one of those travertine stairs made in time past, as its age well demonstrates. The diameter of these stairs is seven palmi. But let us look at a little of the work that Bernini did in the rest of the shafts or areas for the stairs and see if, then, one may, as one can and one must, affirm that, indeed, he brought strength rather than strain or weakness to the ground piers that support the dome.

We can, thus, discover by careful inspection that the previously mentioned shafts are quadrilateral in plan and that they measure nine palmi in length and six and one quarter palmi in width. In order to provide in this space the elements needed to complete the stairways giving access to the upper niches such as had earlier been envisaged, they were built in the exact manner and measure of the first old stairway that leads to the niche containing the Sacred Sudarium. These stairways have a diameter of seven palmi while the length of the shaft is nine palmi. All this clearly shows that the stairs were as much in order as the niches were. So, at one stroke, two most serious lies are exposed: one that the shafts were made by Bernini, and the other that the work done on his order caused strain and weakness to the piers. We can, on the contrary, affirm that by filling in the stairwell shaft by two palmi from the floor of the church up to the upper niches the piers were somewhat strengthened.

From what we have pointed out up to now it already begins to become clear how improper and, indeed, intolerable was that other charge made against Bernini—that of having excavated the corridors that lead from the spiral stairways to the upper niches. It is not easy to imagine that those skillful architects who made shafts for the spiral stairways and shafts leading from those stairwells to the niches had not also left room for such an essential purpose.

But how are we to respond to the other objection of our opponents concerning the incisions they assert Bernini made to provide for the stairs that descend from the floor of the church to the four chapels under the niches? They said the same thing about all these incisions that they said concerning the other undertakings mentioned a little earlier—that they had done great harm to the dome.

Since reason is the only defense against all these calumnies, one need only avail oneself of it in order to respond adequately to all of them, including this last one which is also completely false as we will now see. In Maderno's printed plan of St. Peter's we see in No. 34 the following legend which reads: *Stair, that descends to the confession and to the grottoes at the beginning of the north transept.* Observe the plan and note that this is the stairway behind the statue of St. Longinus.

No. 65 reads: *Stairway by which one descends to the confession and the grottoes;* and this is located behind the statue of St. Andrew.

It is true that two other stairs descending to the grottoes were made later in duplication of the first two and for that purpose the pier wall was cut on a slope large enough to accommodate the stairways. In short the stairs were made in the manner that we see them today. Thus, is it not obvious to anyone who understands architecture that these stairs could not provoke any damage even if the incisions had penetrated to the roots of the foundations, since these stairways are in direct alignment with the niche openings which rise to a height of about forty-eight palmi. Moreover, the stairs were built in such a manner that the piers and the niches both retain their original solidity.

Even before the time of Urban VIII the administrators of the Fabbrica of St. Peter's recognized that stairways must be built in those places. This is clearly revealed by a decree found in the archives of the Holy Congregation of the Fabbrica dated June 3, 1626 and by a note of July 15 of the same year. These documents show that there were already two stairways leading down to the confession and the grottoes. There were also two altars with stone decorations for the celebration of the Mass. The decree also states that another two altars had to be built on the opposite sides. Here are the words of the decree: *Preliminary work is underway for the two altars that are to be built—one under the niche of the Sacred Sudarium and the other under the niche of St. Andrew. After discussing the matter with the Pope it seems most convenient to build in those places the altars of the Sacred Sudarium and of St. Andrew, since there does not now exist any altar where one may celebrate Mass in the places where those relics are conserved.* A postscript adds, "*Fiat verbum cum Sanctissimo.*"

The entry of July 15 of the same year reads as follows: *Concerning the altars of the Sacred Sudarium and of St. Andrew which seemed to him should be erected in those places etc. I am to find out if there are relics of apostles in St. Peter's worthy of accompanying the head of St. Andrew and the head of St. Luke.*

Here then we see indisputably demonstrated with what lack of experience both the common people and the adversaries of Bernini formulated their opinions—those on the one side being as false as those on the other—and by what hollow vanities they were motivated. Since nothing can grow on barren ground, it seems to me that we may well add that the consequences of these charges amounted to nothing. All the additional conjectures were likewise completely futile, as we shall now attempt to show.

Next, they went on to say that an iron chain had been made to encircle the columns and the lantern of the dome. Oh, what fine censure that was, as if the damage to the dome that they had falsely said had been caused by the foundations, would have immediately manifested its effects in the lantern, and that the only remedy for this damage was the remedy offered. To me that is exactly like saying that for the medication of dropsy of the lung the bathing of the finger tip in rose water suffices.

The thunderbolts that fall from the clouds do not journey

toward us so swiftly and so quietly that everyone cannot see and hear them, even those from far away. Nor are people so stolid that when the blows strike they do not move and, indeed, shout and make noise. Therefore, Bernini's attackers must have known of the incident of the thunderbolt that struck the dome shortly before the reinforcements were completed. The bolt, in striking four of the columns of the lantern, not only moved them out of line but also knocked one of the Ionic capitals to the ground. As a result it was necessary to have four iron bands put on the columns so they would make no further movement and a new capital had to be made to take the place of the one shattered by the lightning.

It is shameful to have to respond to the intolerable absurdity that later was uttered. It was said that after the aforesaid work had been done on the lantern it was seen that the dome had, nevertheless, moved and that it was necessary to reinforce it as well with iron bands—a lie truly so gross and monstrous that one would have to say that the dome itself encircled by those people with those imaginary bands would be smaller in comparison. But, yet, we must not remain silent about it. There was never an architect, feeble though he might be, who did not know it is impossible to raise a structure of such a form and size without reinforcing it with chains in many places, just as that great dome was reinforced with chains in two places at the time it was built. I, myself, have been taken up there many times with the drawings and plans in my hand. I have seen it all with my own eyes in the presence of some of the leading architects of Rome. What is more, is not the first precept that our architects are given in the construction of a building of this type their strengthening by means of such reinforcements? But let us look into the smallest details.

The first ring, or we should say the first great iron chain, circles the dome passing under the stairs. The other chain is located at the spring of the dome. We can see that the bolts locking them in position have remained intact from the time of their placement, and they are in exact alignment with the midpoint of the oculus above. They still retain the same rough plaster with which they were covered from the beginning and with which all the other old walls are covered. It is well known among architects that a wall has a certain inherent quality that, when integrated with an ancient wall, is still quite recognizable even after hundreds of years. The reasons for this are so numerous that for the sake of brevity I will pass over them. Who is so scatterbrained that he cannot understand that if these great chains had to be inserted sometime after the dome was built, it would have been necessary to cut into the wall or at least into the surface. Yet we see that not even the surface of the plaster has been altered a jot. The surfaces immediately around the bolts and nuts are well fitted and well preserved. In short, it is all so easy to recognize that either no one who spoke against Bernini saw it or those who saw it and spoke did not comprehend or understand what they saw.

But what will those people say when they finally see what, in order to clear up their errors, we searched for and found in the archives? We found proof that those chains were put around the dome in the pontificate of Sixtus V in the month of April of 1591. And with that nothing more need be said.

Although I had imagined that I had brought the discussion to an end, I find myself only a little further on than I was in the beginning, since I hear many saying that up till now I have not mentioned the crack in the dome. Since this crack is, indeed, real and visible to everyone, it cannot be kept hidden for any reason. And as there is never an effect without a cause, it is necessary to state that this crack also had a cause. To remove suspicion we must demonstrate what this cause was.

First of all it should be recognized that long experience has taught us that all these and similar buildings which have not been reinforced are naturally under strong pressure to move toward the center because of the pressure of the lantern which weighs heavily on them. This is what good architects call the settling of a building. But because of the bands or chains that tightly gird the dome, they have great resistance to this pressure. The force which produces disintegration in the body of buildings by the continuous thrust of its immense weight would be still greater if any of the reinforcing chains were to be wrenched away.

The primary cause of such fissures is, as we said, the weight and the thrust of the building. Ordinarily there is also another cause, that is, the adjustment of the disposition of the masonry mass because of defects due to the workers' lack of skill. Each small negligence in the care of the materials may bring about this damage. Since, as I said, it is an unquestioned principle that buildings never move or produce fissures except in their weakest part, it follows that such movement or fissure cannot occur except in that place where the material is most fragile and not well kept.

I said that not one building of this sort could ever be found which in settling itself and taking hold did not produce some fissures. Evidence of this is found in the dome of S. Maria in Vallicella, called the Chiesa Nuova; in the dome of the Gesù, which settled at the time it was painted; in S. Carlo al Corso; in S. Andrea in Piazza Navona; and, most recently, in the building at Montefiascone. And, moreover, in St. Peter's itself all the domes of the chapels also have cracks, and in the chapel where the mosaics are the cracks, even though covered, are recognizable. And what shall we say of the dome of our cathedral in Florence? Is it perhaps free of this misfortune? No, from earliest times some hair line cracks were to be seen. What we have said about the dome applies as well to other types of vaulting. There are cracks in the vaults of the crossing and the nave and side aisles of the Florence cathedral. Such cracks, whether large or small, are to be found everywhere. In order to avoid such cracks it would be necessary that buildings of this type be constructed in such a manner that all the material used be completely uniform and prepared, baked, and cared for in the same way. Thus, all the bricks would be perfectly aligned and would constitute a solid mass, all of a piece and of unified solidity. The building, then, would stand absolutely rigid, granting there were no defects in the foundations. In such a situation we would find very different results than those we see in the dome of St. Peter's in Rome.

When one is given these as facts, as, indeed, are all of those things we have related, it is not, then, surprising that the great dome of St. Peter's, in settling as it did in time, revealed in the interior some manifestations of movement or small fissures—those, in short, which are seen there and which for greater clarity we will describe as follows.

A very old fissure is visible in the midsection of the dome. It is about an inch wide in the interior and is on a line with the niche containing the Sacred Sudarium. It extends upward but does not, however, reach the lantern opening or, as we say, the oculus. Its lower extremity does not even reach the circuit of the great cornice. Instead, it ends above the capital of the pilaster of the drum.

Nor can anyone say that this crack occurred after the work ordered by Urban VIII and, even less, that it has grown larger in recent years. This is so, not only because of the reasons given earlier, but for many other reasons as well. It is a well-known and proven fact that due to the great torches that through the years were used in the basilica the crack has been exposed to so much smoke that it has become almost black. I said through the years, since functions which require the use of such torches in the church are not so frequent that this smoke blackening could have occurred in a brief period. Moreover, it is known that connoisseurs and lovers of the arts are not lacking in Rome. They affirm that the crack was observed, just as we see it today, with some curiosity forty or fifty years ago. Besides, on the outer part of the wall where the stairs rise up into the body of the dome between the inner and outer domical shells at the point corresponding to the crack, it is clearly discernible that in the very separation all the bricks are flat and level, without one or the other being lower, and the joinings between them are all on a straight line. And what plainer sign can there be for those who have a clear understanding of these problems that this damage does not come from any source other than from the quality of the material which, either because it was badly made or badly maintained, fell when the building settled? In the course of inspections made in St. Peter's in my presence, tests were made which demonstrated that the dome could not have shifted position in recent times. Halfway up we see that the rings and bolts with plaster around them are undisturbed. Nor is there any doubt that if the dome had made any new movement it would have forced the encircling chains out of line and the following effects would have necessarily been produced. First of all, the bolts driven into the eyes of the upper half of these chains or belts or rings, whatever we call them, would have gone out of alignment. The plaster around them, being very weak, would have fallen, as would also the mortar wedges behind the bolts. The iron wedges would have loosened and some of the rings of the chain would also have broken. The mosaic covering the dome on the interior is composed, as we know, of tiny pieces. In the area about the fissure these pieces would have fallen. The same thing would also have happened to the stucco mouldings around the mosaic panels. There would have been many other manifestations, none of which are to be seen in this case.

We can see one of the chains partly uncovered, as it extends down to the floor of the stairs which begins the ascent into the body of the dome. It extends along the side of the wall the thickness of a brick laid edgewise, that is, about three inches. This wall is composed of plain mortar and planking for pointing. This alone, without anything else, demonstrates the falsity of the proposition that the dome is moving or that it has made any movement other than it made in the beginning. There is no brain so thick that it cannot understand clearly that, if even a small tremor occurred in that long iron chain, this very thin wall, which is not even bound in by iron, would have fallen in a minute. But let us note that there could be only two reasons that could cause the dome to move. Either the dome could have pushed outward at the springing where the body commences its thrust, which would necessarily have caused the chains to move. Or the foundation could have given way, which would have caused some of the four piers (which carry the four arches that sustain the dome) to sink. This certainly would have caused ruptures in the whole fabric of the two arches which rest on these piers. Moreover, cracks and fissures would have appeared in the two vaults, that is, the vault of the side aisle and that of the nave. A crack would have appeared along the side of the lateral tribunes, and the dome itself would have displayed other very great signs across its whole breadth, as skillful architects well know. But we see nothing of these signs, nor have we ever seen them. It must be stated, then, that the dome has made no movement except in its earliest period, nor can it do so in the future.

It is false to say that the small crack which is seen in the body of the dome over the niche of St. Longinus, which runs between one dome and the other and can scarcely be seen from the inside of the church, is new. On close observation, we see that it has become blackened with smoke like the other one. Moreover, it does not continue or extend except intermittently in a few places, and it ends in the body of the dome.

Great studies, conducted in the manner followed by Giovan Battista della Porta, formerly architect of the Fabbrica of St. Peter's, on the constitution of the dome have made it clear that the dome inevitably must remain immobile and produce no fissures that could lead to its collapse. But since it would take too long to state here all the reasons and demonstrations, it will be the task of the valorous Mattia de' Rossi to impart this knowledge to anyone experienced in the fine arts who wishes it.

Bernini's adversaries exhausted themselves in stating and asserting that today the dome shows other cracks in its body in the part toward the church, under the small arches of the lantern, and in the arches which pass under the ribs of the passageway that goes between the inner and outer walls. Such statements are no less futile than the other allegations. One understands their emptiness when one has the knowledge that these cracks were always to be seen there. But ask those persons what it is that they call a crack and what, according to the best and surest rules of architecture, are the causes responsible for such hairline cracks in buildings. Have they perhaps stripped or knocked the plaster off that section of the wall in order to gain sufficient knowledge to give a considered opinion of the condition? Yet it is absolutely true that without such diligence it is not so simple for anyone to arrive at the truth. If they would like to find out from one who has taken the proper steps and closely surveyed the whole thing what those hairline cracks are, especially those which extend under the lesser vault, those seen in front of the small arcades, as well as the crack in the church under the impost of the arch which provides decoration and comes out over the projection of the two pilasters at the entrance to the tribune of St. Simon and St. Jude, I shall now give an explanation of them.

It is, first of all, advisable that they should realize that if any vault in the form of an arch of bricks is constructed with such care that each brick is directly aligned with the center, then, each brick will, by reason of the union of its strength, be more tightly bound to the others, instead of falling under pressure. This is so true, that if an arch is made in the dry manner, that is without mortar, and if its abutments are proportionately resistant to its force, it would never have a crack of any kind, nor would it by itself undergo any movement. This is such a well-known principle that not only the architect and the mason but even the ordinary worker knows and understands it. But if it should happen that the person constructing the arch, through negligence, did not lay the bricks in such a manner that they all converge on a central point, then, as soon as the centering is taken down, the arch will have to settle and find a new sustaining point. All the bricks correctly aligned with the central point will press together toward it, forming a rupture which the other bricks will fill. When there is a disjunction between one brick and another, there will always be a great thickness of mortar which will produce a crack in the same manner as the first movement. The crack will be transmitted to the exterior plaster on the sides and underneath to the extent of the width of the arch. On this point see Fig. 9.

These, then, are the cracks that we see in the corridor which runs between the two shells in the body of the dome. They are seen also under one of the small arches of the little corridors which go around the lantern between the two walls of the drum.

Did not the same thing happen to the underside of the arch of the tribune called the tribune of St. Simon and St. Jude, where the hairline crack extends along the whole length and appears outside in the stucco decorations? Go around the underside of the arch below the vault of the church and make a survey up to the projection of the pilasters. Then, having made a thorough examination underneath and from the top of the great cornice, and from the inside of the church, you will see that the crack is only in the part below where the decorations and the ornamentations are. The upper part is seen to be good, completely sound, and with no trace of fissure. The fissure appears only in the stucco decorations. Its appearance there is due solely to the workers' negligence in the conservation of the materials of which the decorations are composed.

Anyone who has the most elementary understanding of these arts will see clearly that the few other small cracks that can be perceived on the frames which provide adornment for the long panels in the inside of the dome, where the mosaic angels are, and directly above the frames of the tondi, where the seraphim are, derive from causes which I shall here make clear to the satisfaction of the least informed. When the stucco worker makes his models in rough plaster, he also makes an armature of studs; plaster is then added for grooving. In the process of this work it sometimes happens, particularly when the job is vast, that some small pieces fall off when the plaster is left to set. It then is necessary to patch up those small sections. The stucco worker covers the area with stucco or plaster or marble dust and pulls the molds. In the process of the drying of the whole, that area which had to be patched, being fresher than the other sections, necessarily forms a small crack, which is transmitted to the exterior where it remains always. It cannot properly be termed a crack, as it is not in the heart of the structure but entirely on the outside in the decorative overlay appended to it. Hairline cracks of this sort which weave in and out, forming various odd patterns, are frequently seen in the vaults of buildings. They are not given the appellation of crack by architects, since they come from too hastily applying the first rough coat of plaster, the grooving, the plastering of the vault surfaces, one over the other without allowing proper time for setting. However, experience teaches us that when these vaults are stripped they are found to be sound and without fissures in any part.

I am pleased to present these proofs. They represent only a small number of the proofs that could be drawn from the extensive fine material that Mattia de' Rossi, that most expert architect, presented in conformity with the strict terms of his profession. Through his studies anyone who wishes may at his pleasure discover how improper and damaging to the fame of another is the discussion of the works of great masters by those who do not know and do not understand; and how vain and ridiculous it is, without the testimony of a knowledgeable eye, to give judgment on rumormongerings, running after idle reports.

STATEMENT OF THE AUTHOR

It is well known that in the natural world, those things that are less useful to our life or less valuable to us because of their insignificant qualities, are most numerous; while, on the other hand, those things which for the benefits they bring humanity and for all their other important attributes are held, by common consent, to be worthy of all esteem are very few. Thus, it is not altogether improper to affirm that the number of men of marvelous talent, in comparison to those not so endowed, is so small and dispersed that, rather than every generation, scarcely every century can succeed in possessing one. If, as it sometimes happens, Heaven favors us with such a one, we soon see, thanks to his great and notable deeds, that the world seems happier and more beautiful, and we also see buds bursting forth everywhere from the scattered seeds of his famous works, so that the Kingdom of Virtue becomes, so to speak, suddenly rich. However, in spite of human wishes, even for such men time flows so quickly and elusively that, finally, they are also led to the fatal hour. It is thus inevitable that those who poured forth such benefits through the long course of years should be lost in an instant. In such cases human ingenuity knows no better way to make its affliction more bearable than by putting on paper the memory of their virtues, venturing at the same time to transmit them to a wide audience, and, by the recounting of these virtues, to bring enjoyment to future generations and to enkindle in every heart a desire to imitate them.

And from that I derive the motive for my conviction that he who undertakes to relate the deeds of virtuous men cannot prescribe any other goal for himself than to attempt, as far as he is able, to proceed in such a way that he, let us say, re-creates them, so that the reader turns from reading the accounts with, if not the same effects, at least with effects very similar to those I described earlier. That is to say, such commemorative writing, besides the merit of giving virtue its due, makes the world glad for the memory of it, as well as making courageous and magnanimous whoever undertakes, through such efforts, to achieve complete success. Therefore, it may happen that the writer at times discovers among the purest gold some particle that is not completely pure. But the writer must not, because of that, abstain from making the light of that which is most perfect shine forth for everyone's eyes, since it must be plain that to have in oneself some mixture of clay is only to be human.

With that assumption, it is now worthwhile that I declare to those who shall read the little that I have written, that in order to make the great works of Cavalier Bernini better known, I have undertaken to praise him and nothing more. By so doing I never thought to deserve being considered prejudiced or anything but sincere, since it is most true that in so doing I pledged myself to the above-mentioned aims which I thought I could never achieve in my writings if I had not felt the compulsion to bring to light that which is most beautiful.

I wish to make it clear to everyone that, before setting out to write not only of Bernini but of any celebrated man, I made a pact with my pen that it must, as if it were an amorous bee, follow the trail of the mellifluous parts of the flowers, leaving the opposite course to some poisonous spider, born in filth and nourished by garbage, who now or after I shall have published my account wants to sink his teeth into the less appetizing, from which I kept my respectful lips, and feed upon it. According to rumor, one such has already wished to do so—even as I wrote of this great artist. He struggles to draw from those same shoots from which I extracted the sweetest and gentlest substance some imperfection and then, mixing it with the sordid humor of his own substance, to vomit forth poison. His only prudence lies in not wishing to commit his own name to print (a name still unknown to me) so as not to reap the infamy that such an ugly and detestable labor merits.

Now everyone knows, especially he who entertains such monstrous ideas in his mind, that Heaven in wanting to proclaim to our age the greatness of Bernini did not entrust such a judgment to ill-bred men but wished his acclamation to come from those in high positions. And, in fact, his glories began in his earliest youth with the plaudits of Rome in the holy habitations of the high pontiffs. There they were raised and nourished until Europe and, one could almost say, the whole world was full of them. There was not a great master or pontiff or king or great monarch who, on the basis of the living testimony of his works, did not with many signal acts subscribe to the general judgment. All of which suffices for me to show without any fear this great genius always as himself. Such will be my sentiment in anything I might say of any other most extraordinary master of the fine arts. If such had not been and would not in the future be my intention, I do not know how I should ever have the courage to call myself a son of the most noble and most virtuous Accademia della Crusca, which is always a friend of men of high virtue. In exploring their valuable works, the Academy practices compassion in what it perceives has not reached the greatest perfection and only

IL PIU BEL FIORE NE COGLIE.

CATALOGUE

In order not to extend the narrative tediously and fragment the account by recounting one by one all of Bernini's works, even the most minute, it pleased me to gather them all together in an exact record in accordance with the information that I received in Rome from one who has complete knowledge of them. I believe that such a record will, in fact, be very clear and satisfactory to those who read it. It is as follows:

PORTRAIT BUSTS*

Majordomo of Sixtus V	*S. Prassede*
Giovanna Vigena	*S. Maria sopra Minerva*
Cardinal Delfino	*Venice*
The same in profile	*Venice*
Cardinal Serdi	*Paris*
Cardinal Valiero	*Venice*
Cardinal Montalto	*Casa Peretti*
Monsignor del Pozzo	. . . .
Monsignor Francesco Barberino, uncle of Urban VIII	*Casa Barberina*
The mother of Urban VIII	*Casa Barberina*
The father of Urban VIII	*Casa Barberina*
D. Lucrezia Barberina	*Casa Barberina*
Two of Pope Urban VIII	*Casa Barberina*
The same	*Casa Barberina*
Another in bronze	*Casa Barberina*

* Baldinucci's spelling of proper names has been retained.

Monsignor Montoia	*S. Jacopo degli Spagnuoli*
Pope Paul V *Cardinal Scipione Borghese*	*Villa Borghese*
Another of the same Cardinal	*Casa Borghese*
Urban VIII	*Casa Giori*
Another in bronze	*Abate Braccesi*
Don Paolo Giordano, Duke of Bracciano	*Casa Orsina*
Costanza Piccolomini	*Gallery of the Grand Duke*
Innocent X	*Casa Panfilia*
The same	*For Casa Bernina*
Gregory XV *Another in bronze*	*Casa Ludovisi*
Alexander VII *The same*	*Casa Chigi*
The same	*For Casa Bernina*
Cardinal di Richelieu	*Paris*
Charles I, King of England	*London*
Francesco, Duke of Modena	*Modena*
Don Carlo Barberino	*Capitoline*
Louis XIV, King of France	*Paris*
Clement X	. . . .
An English Knight	*London*

MARBLE STATUES

Cardinal Bellarmino	*The Gesù*
Allegory of Religion	*The Gesù (decorations for Cardinal Bellarmino's tomb)*
Paul V	*The Gesù*
Aeneas, Anchises and Ascanius	*Villa Borghese*
Rape of Proserpina	*Villa Ludovisi*
David *Apollo and Daphne*	*Villa Borghese*

Work	Location
Neptune and Glaucus	*Villa Montalto*
St. Lawrence on the gridiron	*Villa Strozzi*
St. Sebastian	*Casa Barberina*
St. Sebastian	*Princess Rossano*
St. Bibiana	*S. Bibiana*
Angel on the tomb of Card. Delfino	*Venice*
St. Longinus	*S. Pietro in Vaticano*
Head and model of the statue of Countess Matilda	*S. Pietro in Vaticano*
Allegory of Charity *Allegory of Justice*	*Tomb of Urban VIII*
Equestrian statue of Constantine	*Portico, S. Pietro in Vaticano*
Triton in the Navona Fountain	*Opposite Palazzo Panfilio*
Rock mass for the fountain in Piazza Navona *Horse* *Lion*	*Piazza Navona*
Truth	*Casa Bernina*
St. Jerome in the Chigi Chapel	*Siena*
Daniel *Habakkuk and the Angel*	*Chigi Chapel, S. Maria del Popolo*
Urban VIII	*Capitoline*
Gabriele Fonseca holding rosary	*S. Lorenzo in Lucina*
The last Cardinal Cornaro	*S. Maria della Vittoria*
The Angel with the superscription	*Ponte S. Angelo*
The Angel with the crown of thorns *Another with the superscription*	*For Casa Rospigliosi*
Head of the anima beata *Head of the* anima dannata	*S. Jacopo degli Spagnuoli*
Angel above the high altar *Another in the same location*	*S. Agostino in Rome*
Bas-relief of Christ and St. Peter commonly called Pasce oves meas	*S. Pietro in Vaticano, above central door*

Work	Location
Colossus of Louis XIV, King of France	*For His Most Christian Majesty*
The Triton in the Barberini Fountain	*Piazza Barberina*
The Blessed Lodovica Albertoni	*S. Francesco a Ripa*
Tomb of Alexander VII with his and other statues	*S. Pietro in Vaticano*
The Saviour, Bernini's last work	*For Her Majesty the Queen of Sweden*
Up to 15 heads	*Various places*

STATUES IN METAL

<table>
<tr><td>Silver bust of St. Eustace</td><td>S. Eustachio</td></tr>
<tr><td>Urban VIII</td><td>Velletri</td></tr>
<tr><td>Statue of Urban VIII for his tomb</td><td>S. Pietro in Vaticano</td></tr>
<tr><td>Allegory of Death on tomb of Urban VIII</td><td>S. Pietro in Vaticano</td></tr>
<tr><td>Four metal angels for the ciborium</td><td rowspan="7">S. Pietro in Vaticano</td></tr>
<tr><td>The Four Doctors of the Church for the Cathedra Petri</td></tr>
<tr><td>The throne for the Cathedra Petri</td></tr>
<tr><td>Angel at the throne</td></tr>
<tr><td>Angel at the throne</td></tr>
<tr><td>Two angels above the throne</td></tr>
<tr><td>Large angel in the Glory</td></tr>
<tr><td>Crucifix, life-size, for the altar of Philip IV's Royal Chapel</td><td>Madrid</td></tr>
<tr><td>St. Francesca Romana, angel and tomb</td><td>S. Francesca Romana</td></tr>
<tr><td>Two metal angels on the ciborium of Chapel of the Holy Sacrament</td><td>S. Pietro in Vaticano</td></tr>
<tr><td>Portrait of Cardinal di Richelieu</td><td>Paris</td></tr>
</table>

CATALOGUE

WORKS OF ARCHITECTURE AND VARIED WORKS

The facade, stairway and hall of Palazzo Barberino
Palazzo Lodovisi—not completed
The Novitiate Church of the Jesuit Fathers
The Church in Ariccia
The Church with dome in Castel Gandolfo
The gallery and facade facing the sea of the palace at Castel Gandolfo
The Cornaro Chapel in S. Maria della Vittoria
The Chapel of Cardinal de Silva at S. Isidoro
The Allaleona Chapel in S. Domenico di Montemagnanapoli
The Raimondi Chapel in S. Pietro a Montorio
The Siri Chapel in Savona
Tomb of Alexander VII in S. Pietro in Vaticano
Ciborium of metal and lapis lazuli in the Chapel of the Holy Sacrament in S. Pietro in Vaticano
The four angels in S. Pietro in Vaticano where the relics are kept—from the cornice to the floor.
The baldacchino or four columns in S. Pietro in Vaticano
The Cathedra Petri
The Tomb of Countess Matilda in S. Pietro in Vaticano
The stairway of the Vatican Palace
The tomb of Urban VIII in S. Pietro in Vaticano
Portico in Piazza S. Pietro
The Merenda Memorial in S. Lorenzo in Damaso
A similar one in the Convertite
Suor Maria Raggi Memorial in S. Maria sopra Minerva
The tomb of Cardinal Pimentelli in S. Maria sopra Minerva
Arch and decoration of the Vatican Ducal Stairs
Alexander VII's addition to the Quirinal Palace
The fountain in Piazza Navona and the obelisk
The restoration of the Chigi Chapel in S. Maria del Popolo
The restoration of the entire church of S. Maria del Popolo
The Porta del Popolo from the cornice upward

State rooms with loggia of Clement IX in the Quirinal Palace
Statuary decorations for Ponte di S. Angelo
Civitavecchia Arsenal
Villa for the Rospigliosi family in Pistoia
Altar for the Rospigliosi Gesù Chapel in Pistoia
Lower altar for tomb of S. Francesca Romana
Altar in S. Calisto
High altar in S. Lorenzo in Damaso
The facade and restoration of S. Bibiana
The fountain in Piazza Barberina
Marble putti and medallion decorations in the lateral pilasters of S. Pietro in Vaticano with the arms of Innocent X
The arms of Innocent X with statues and other decorations of the columns of cottanello in S. Pietro in Vaticano
Lantern and ordering of the dome of S. Maria di Montesanto
Pavement for S. Pietro in Vaticano, commissioned by Innocent X
Pavement of the Colonnade, commissioned by Clement X

(I have not included scenery, a forty hours' devotion, fireworks, catafalques, masques, and similar things.)

LAUS DEO